SWING TRADING

Tips and Tricks, Best Techniques and Principles, Advanced and Effective Strategies to Execute Swing Trading

WILLIAM RILEY

TABLE OF CONTENTS

SWING TRADING

*Tips and Tricks to Learn and Execute
Swing Trading Strategies to Get Started*

SWING TRADING

Best Techniques and Principles to Execute Swing Trading Strategies

SWING TRADING

Advanced and Effective Strategies to Execute Swing Trading

SWING TRADING

*Tips and Tricks to Learn
and Execute Swing Trading Strategies
to Get Started*

WILLIAM RILEY

Introduction

One of the best ways to make a lot of money without having to slave oneself away is through trading of financial securities like stocks, bonds, currencies, etc. There are many ways to do it, but one of the most popular ways is Swing Trading.

What is Swing Trading? How does it work? You'll get to learn the answers to these questions and more in this book. After you've finished reading it, you'll be in a very good position to take further action with regard to starting your very first Swing Trade.

So, shall we begin? Turn the page and let's start!

Chapter 1

Swing Trading: What Is It?

Swing trading refers to an investing strategy where investment positions are maintained for more than 24 hours. The underlying belief of this strategy is that significant changes in a company's performance and financial condition usually take several days to substantially impact the prices of financial assets and generate acceptable profits.

With swing trading, traders try to earn significant profits from meaningful price changes in a financial asset's price, such as shares of stocks or bonds, over a longer period than day trading but within a much shorter time frame than a buy-and-hold strategy. The primary analysis tool swing traders use is technical analysis, while some combine fundamental analysis with technical analysis to narrow down the range of financial securities to swing trade.

Swing traders take and hold one of two types of positions, long or short, for more than 24 hours. Normally, the longest time they hold their positions is a couple of months. But some swing trading positions can last longer.

Swing trading has one very specific goal, which is to ride the wave of promising price moves. Swing traders may be high-risk takers, trading very volatile financial assets like stocks and cryptocurrencies, to make very good profits in shorter periods of time. They may also be a bit more conservative, choosing to swing trade less volatile financial securities and don't mind waiting for a couple of weeks or months for major price swings to take advantage of.

Regardless of one's risk tolerance and preference, swing traders aim to time their positions shortly before their anticipated price swings in order to profit much from such substantial price changes.

What separates swing traders from buy-and-hold or long-term investors is they aren't interested in getting huge chunks or the entire chunk of a financial security's expected long-term price move. They're only interested in capturing a chunk of the entire pie via relatively shorter holding positions. Once they do, they move on to the next swing trading opportunity.

Some of the most important things to keep in mind about swing trading include:

1. Swing trades typically take several days up to several months to come full circle, i.e., generate profits;

2. Swing traders face overnight and weekend risks, i.e., the risk that the next trading day's prices of financial securities can open at a substantially different price than its previous close; and

3. Swing traders typically use set trading parameters to trigger trading actions such as stop-loss and profit targets, price chart patterns, technical indicators, etc.

Choosing Trades

One of the ways swing traders choose which financial securities to swing trade and when to swing trade is the risk-reward ratio. For example, swing traders will not hesitate to swing a trade a stock they believe has a risk-reward ratio of 1:3, i.e., a $1 investment can potentially result in a $3 profit in a couple of days, weeks, or months.

Swing traders usually avoid financial securities they believe to only have a risk-reward ratio of 1:1 or worse, 1: less-than-one.

Another method by which swing traders choose financial securities for trading is technical analysis. Technical analysis involves studying the price movements of financial securities alone. No financial statements. No economic developments. It just takes into consideration price movements, which are believed to contain all possible information about financial securities.

Technical analysis answers the questions when to buy and when to sell. Technical analysis can be grouped into two main categories: price chart patterns and technical indicators. We'll discuss these in greater detail in the subsequent **Chapters.**

Another way swing traders choose their swing-trading financial securities is fundamental analysis. This type of analysis involves looking at a company's financial data and information, among other important information that can affect its financial condition and profitability. Fundamental analysis primarily answers two questions:

1. What is a financial security's true financial worth based on financial and economic data; and

2. Based on a financial security's market price, is said security over-priced or under-valued? If over-priced, sell. If under-valued, buy.

Because swing trading is about timing and not actual value, swing traders use technical analysis over fundamental analysis. However, some traders use fundamental analysis to short-list their swing trading candidates. Fundamental analysis tells them which financial securities have the potential for major price swings based on actual value and technical analysis helps them to time their swing trades on such securities.

Pros and Cons of Swing Trading

One of the main advantages of swing trading is that it doesn't require as much time to execute as day trades. This is because swing trading requires opening and closing positions over a period of several days, at the minimum. Day trading involves opening and closing multiple trades within the day that generate small profits, i.e., more voluminous and time consuming.

Another is that swing trading can help traders/investors optimize their short-term trading income potential by identifying and riding much of a security's or the market's price swings. By waiting for several days for major price swings to happen, swing traders are able to minimize the number of their trades and save on transactions costs, i.e., buying and selling a financial security only once over several days in which prices swing generously. Day trading on the other hand, liquidates positions quickly, often with small profits and more transactions costs.

The last advantage associated with swing trading is simplicity. Because it relies mostly on technical analysis to time trades, which requires price data only, there's no need for very complex analysis or hard-to-get financial or economic information.

One of the issues many traders have with swing trading, especially the day traders, is overnight risk exposure, at the shortest. Depending on the financial security in one's holdings and the expected risk-reward ratio, swing trading puts traders' positions at risk for several days, weeks, or even months.

Another potential disadvantage of swing trading is that substantial price swings can substantially increase one's potential trading losses. While prices of financial securities can skyrocket within a few days, they can also plummet within the same short period of time.

And finally, the much shorter time frame of swing trading can put investors at risk of missing out on potentially greater gains over the long term. For swing traders, however, the bird in the hand is better than the one in the bush, as the saying goes. They'd rather lock in on smaller profits now than risk waiting for potentially larger price increases over longer periods of time.

The Difference between Swing Trading and Day Trading

As you may have already noticed, the primary difference between swing and day trading is time frame or position-holding period. Day trading positions are opened and closed within the same day, hence the name. Swing trading, on the other hand, closes positions within a few days, weeks, or even months.

Another difference between the two is basis for closing positions. Day traders' primary basis for closing their positions is end of day, regardless of whether doing so will be profitable. Day traders are happy with even just a few ticks' worth of profits because they trade more frequently, which can lead to substantial accumulations in small trading profits. The important thing is their positions are closed by the end of the trading day.

Swing traders, on the other hand, are more concerned with price movements, i.e., substantial price swings, rather than time. That's why they don't mind maintaining positions for several days, weeks, or even months. Meaningful price swings, not just ticks, don't happen intraday or even overnight. They take some time.

Another difference between the two is risk tolerance. Day traders aren't comfortable dealing with overnight risks for meaningful price gaps in the following trading morning's opening prices. Hence, they're hell-bent on closing positions by end of day, profits or not.

Swing traders, on the other hand, are comfortable with such risks. Heck, they're even comfortable with risks that can span several weeks or months. Again, it's because they're more after the meaningful price swings rather than just small price ticks. And meaningful price swings take time to happen.

Because swing traders are more focused on being able to ride the wave of potentially significant price swings, they don't need to hold positions as large as day traders. To give you a clearer picture of what this means, consider the following example.

Swing trader Jack takes a position in 1,000 shares of stock of Company A at $10-per-share with the intention of waiting for a $5 or 50% upward price swing in the next few weeks or months. This means he's looking to earn $5,000 on his trading position of $10,000 in the next few weeks or months.

Day trader Jill also wants to earn about $5,000 by trading stocks of Company A. But being a day trader, the trading horizon is within 1 day only. A 50% change in a stock's price is highly unlikely which means Jill will have to settle for a much smaller price change – ticks, to be more specific – to generate the same $5,000.

Let's say that on average, the average intraday upward price tick of Company A's stocks is $0.05. This means if day trader Jill wants to earn about $5,000 day trading Company A's stocks at $10 per share, she'll need to buy:

$5,000 ÷ $0.05 = $1,000,000.00

To generate the same $5,000 day trading at an average intraday upward price tick of $0.05 per share, day trader Jill would need to take a $1 million position on Company A's stocks, which she'll need to close within the day.

Choosing Stocks to Swing Trade

Picking the right stocks is crucial for swing trading success. While there are no sure-ball and hard-and-fast rules for choosing winning stocks for swing trading, the most ideal stocks for swing trading are stocks of companies with the biggest market capitalizations. Why?

First, the fact that they have the biggest market capitalizations imply that they're the most financially sound companies on an exchange, e.g., the NYSE and NASDAQ. And by virtue of being so, they will also tend to be the most actively traded shares on such exchanges.

One of the benefits of the most actively traded stocks in on any exchange is that their prices tend to exhibit meaningful but often predictable swings. In a sense, they have lower risks for loss because such stocks usually trade within an identifiable price band.

This is why swing traders may be able to optimize their profits and minimize their risks using fundamental analysis. This type of analysis can help identify shares of stock with solid underlying fundamentals, which provide technical analysis a solid basis for reading how the market will act on certain financial securities.

When to Swing Trade

The worst time to do swing trades or take swing-trade positions is during extreme markets, i.e., a bear or a bull market. Why?

Remember that while swing trading holds positions significantly longer than day trading, it's not a medium to long terms approach. This means it expects to close positions within a couple of months at the most, preferably within a few days or weeks only. Markets need to be moving sideways, i.e., neither bullish nor bearish.

This is because when securities are in a sideways market, their prices tend to vacillate in an identifiable price range or band, i.e., highs and lows. In a sideways market, prices of securities like stocks or bonds tend to peak and trough at roughly the same prices multiple times within a short period of time. Such predictability provides opportunities for riding significant price swings en route to meaningful swing trading profits.

During bear or bull markets, momentum pushes prices of securities in one direction for an extended period of time, usually many months or several years. Swing trading during such markets won't be optimal because of high transactions costs that result from frequent position taking and closing.

For bull or bear markets, the best approach for optimal profits is taking long positions that ride out these markets. By taking long positions, one eliminates frequent trading as well as the transactions costs associated with them.

However, the primary challenge facing both swing traders and long-term position takers is correctly identifying market trends as quickly as possible. And everybody knows that being able to identify the exact moment when market trends reverse is as reliable as fortune telling. The most reasonable expectation is to be able to minimize the lag time between when markets reverse and catching such reverse. This is why technical analysis is a very important tool in the arsenals of both swing traders and long-term position takers.

Chapter 2

Fundamental versus Technical Analysis

Before getting into the nitty-gritty of technical analysis, it's important to understand both fundamental and technical analysis. One's ability to do so can substantially impact his or her swing trading chances of succeeding and profiting.

Fundamental analysis is a method of analyzing or evaluating financial securities using "fundamental" data, e.g., a company's balance sheet and income statement data, economic data, and political information or developments. Some of the most important questions that fundamental analysis can help answer include:

- What is the objective or true value of a financial security like a share of stock or bonds;

- Is a financial security trading at a discount (buy) or at a premium (sell);

- What is the estimated future value of a financial security based on the issuing entity's (company or government) historical financial data; and

- What is a rational expectation for a financial security's return on investment or ROI?

Basically, fundamental analysis answers the question, which financial securities are worth buying or selling.

Technical Analysis

On the other hand, technical analysis answers only one type of question: the "when" question. When to buy a financial security? When to sell it?

Technical analysis isn't concerned with a financial security's true or intrinsic value. Its only concern is timing of trades.

Technical analysis is much easier to perform than fundamental analysis because it only needs two types of data: historical prices and trading volumes. That's it, no need for financial statements, income statements, management reports, etc. And these can be easily obtained through stock exchanges and other financial market websites like Reuters, Bloomberg, etc.

Why the simplification? Technical analysis relies heavily on the efficient markets hypothesis, which states that possibly obtainable information about a financial security is fully reflected in its market price. As such, why bother computing for or estimating intrinsic value?

In effect, technical analysis is more of a social psychology tool than a statistical one, though technical indicators use statistics to compute for trading indicators and triggers. Why? It's because what technical analysis is really trying to tell traders, swingers or otherwise, is what the collective minds of investors think of a financial security and what they're doing about it. According to technicians, the term used to refer to technical analysis practitioners, prices behave in ways that indicate investors' general sentiments towards a specific financial security or financial market.

There are two ways to perform technical analysis: price chart reading and technical indicators.

Price Charts

Price charts are graphical representations the historical prices of financial securities. When plotted on a chart, the prices form patterns from which technicians glean insights as to how investors in general think and behave about a security or a market.

To the unschooled price charts or graphs look nothing more like a work of abstract art, i.e., it doesn't make much sense. But to seasoned traders, they're like a Picasso!

Historical prices, in general, are believed to exhibit certain shapes or patterns that if one reads correctly, can reveal when a trend will reverse or can be expected to continue. Some of the most common price chart patterns include:

- Head and Shoulders;
- Reverse Head and Shoulders;
- Double Tops
- Double Bottoms;
- Triple Tops;
- Triple Bottoms;
- Flags;
- Wedges; and
- Pennants.

Integral to price chart reading are the concepts of trends, support and resistance. The trend is the general direction of a financial security or financial market's prices, which can be bullish, bearish, or neutral.

Bull markets refer to situations when prices of a financial security or a market are going up. Bear markets refer to a sustained drop in financial security and market prices. Neutral refers to sideways movement of prices, which we identified earlier as the best possible market for swing trading.

Support and resistance are integral parts of established trends. Support price refers to the lowest price at which traders tend to scoop up a financial security and make its price rebound. A support line is a line that connects price chart's support prices, which acts as a boundary from which a security's price bounces back up.

Resistance prices are considered as "ceiling" prices at which traders usually sell off a particular financial security. Once traders sell at the resistance, the price of a particular security goes down. The line that connects a price chart's resistance prices is called the resistance line. Like the support line, the resistance line acts like an upper boundary from which prices of securities usually bounce back down from.

In bull markets, the support line slopes upward. This means that the price at which traders "dump" a particular security increases over time, reflecting a generally bullish sentiment for the security. While it's understood that the resistance line is also sloping upward, the support line is the crucial line here. Why?

The support line represents the lowest price traders are willing to sell a specific security for a period of time. If it's sloping upward, it means that the general sentiment of traders is that the price of that security will continue to go up, hence they unload at higher prices. So when prices drop substantially below the support line, i.e., "breach the line," with abnormally high trading volume, the general sentiment is that a bullish trend has already ended and a bearish one has already begun.

During a bear market or a bearish trend, the important line to watch out for is the resistance line, which is downward sloping. With a downward sloping resistance line, the price at which traders are generally willing to buy a security becomes lower and lower over time, reflecting the belief that the price will continue to go down.

But when the price of a security in a bearish trend exceeds or breaches the resistance line by a substantial margin accompanied by an abnormally high trading volume, it indicates a highly probably trend reversal, i.e., that the security's bullish trend has begun already.

Now, what do support and resistance lines have to do with price patterns? Depending on whether the price pattern is bullish or bearish, breaching of established support and resistance lines signal trend reversals.

But we've talked about how swing trading is more suited for sideways trending securities or markets. What use would the concepts of support and resistance be to swing traders then?

Sideways markets or trends doesn't mean that the price of a security moves perfectly sideways, i.e., unchanging. It changes but the price increases up to a certain upper psychological limit and drops only as low as an established psychological lower limit.

Sounds familiar? Aren't those resistance and support levels? Hence, a sideways trending security or market has a nearly flat-sloping pair of support and resistance lines at the bottom and top of its price fluctuation band, respectively.

The same principle applies to using price charts for swing trading: take positions when prices touch and bounce from the support and resistance lines. In particular, take long position when the price touches and bounces off from the support line and sell when it does the resistance line.

Technical Indicators

These refer to mathematically-processed price data measurements that indicate highly probable trend reversals and continuations. There are two general kinds of technical indicators: leading and lagging.

Leading indicators anticipate or predict where prices of securities will most likely head toward. In other words, leading indicators predict future price directions.

Lagging indicators, on the other hand, identify when an old trend has already ended and a new trend already started. It doesn't predict, but instead, it catches up to something that has already started, hence the term "lagging."

Leading indicators offer traders the benefit of being able to anticipate up-coming trends or reversals and get ahead of the pack when it comes to taking profitable positions. The flip side of this is that there's no such thing as a perfect indicator or statistical prediction model, including leading indicators. This means leading indicators put traders at risks for reading future trends wrong and taking unprofitable positions.

Lagging indicators on the other hand, aren't as risky because by virtue of them lagging behind trend reversals that have already happened, they don't put traders at the same level of risks for misreading trends and unprofitable positions. However, lagging behind prevents traders from making the most out of their profitable trades because trend reversals have already been underway for quite a length of time before they catch them.

Technical indicators can be either of the following:

A) Trend (Lagging): signals when prices are bullish, bearish, or sideways;

B) Mean Reversion (Lagging): estimates the extent of a security's potential price swing before retracement occurs;

C) Relative Strength (Leading): estimates the current buying or selling pressure of a security's price, which are taken as signals of impending trend reversals or continuations;

D) Momentum: estimates the speed at which the price of a security changes over a specific period of time; and

E) Volume (Lagging or Leading): Indicates who's in control of a security's price movements, i.e., bullish or bearish traders.

Fundamental and Technical Analysis: A Synergistic Combo

Most swing traders only use technical analysis for good reason: extensive fundamental analysis is a very tedious process, if only because of the kinds of data or information needed. But swing traders can make their lives easier and increase their chances of making successful swing trades if they incorporate even just a little amount of effort to do fundamental analysis.

How?

Swing traders can use simple fundamental analysis to identify stocks that have solid fundamental underpinnings on which they can use technical analysis to time their swing trades. For example, swing traders can use P/E ratios to shortlist stocks with large market capitalizations and high daily turnovers to monitor for potential swing trading purposes. It's easy to shortlist such stocks using financial market portals like Bloomberg and Reuters within seconds or minutes.

Chapter 3

Technical Analysis:
Popular Chart Patterns

Technical analysis is a method that answers the question of when to take or liquidate positions in markets or financial securities. It does so by analyzing historical prices and trading volumes via price chart patterns and technical measures or indicators.

Technical analysis is grounded on two key assumptions:

A) All possible information that can be gathered about a financial security or market, including financial and economic information, are already reflected on market prices, hence the focus on price;

B) Trading volume is a strong indicator of market interest or disinterest in financial securities;

C) Prices aren't as random as many think they are because it tends to follow general trends; and

D) Because prices follow patterns that tend to repeat themselves over time, traders can learn to anticipate price movements of financial securities with fairly high accuracy.

Types of Price Charts

Price charts presents the historical prices of financial markets or securities over a specific period of time in a graphical way. The three key elements of a price chart include historical prices, trading volumes, and time intervals. Technical analysts rely heavily on price charts that they're also referred to as chartists.

Technical analysis uses different types of price charts, the most popular of which include:

A) Line charts;

B) Bar charts;

C) Candlestick charts;

D) Renko charts;

E) Heikin Ashi charts; and

F) Point-and-Figure charts.

Line Charts

This is the most basic kind of price chart used in technical analysis. It links together closing prices for a chosen period of time, e.g., daily, weekly, monthly, using a line. Because it gives a very general perspective of a market or security price's current and past directions, it's the most common type of chart used in reports and presentations. Traders who believe that the most important or the only relevant price for a period of time is the closing price tend to prefer this type of chart when it comes to using technical analysis, even if the information presented is limited to closing prices only.

Bar Charts

Another basic chart used by technical analysts but compared to line charts, this type of chart provides more price information about a security or a market. In particular, bar charts show historical open, high, low, and closing prices.

This type of price chart uses a series of "crosses," where the vertical lines present the price range for the period (highest and lowest) while the horizontal lines represent the opening (left line) and closing (right line) prices for the period. It's color-coded, too, i.e.:

A) If the closing price is higher than its opening, the line is green or black, which represents an increasing period; and

B) If the closing price is lower than its opening, the line is red, which represents a decreasing period.

Candlestick Charts

As the name suggests, this type of chart represents historical price information in the shape of a candle, i.e., a thick body that represents the opening and closing prices and "wicks" or "shadows" that protrude from above and below, which represent the highest and lowest prices for the period, respectively. When the body is color green or black, it means that its price closed at a higher level than its opening for that period. When the body is red, its price closed lower than the opening one.

Renko Charts

Renko charts a lot different than the first three we talked about in that it focuses only on price movements, to the exclusion of other information like time and trading volumes.

Renko charts use bricks to represent price movements and these bricks are colored white/green and red/black. Their placements are dependent on how their prices moved compared to the previous brick. When the price of the security concerned went up from the previous one, the brick's colored white/green. If it went down from the previous, the color is red/black.

New price "bricks" are created and placed in the chart only after meeting a specific volatility condition, which results in either a major advantage or disadvantage for investors and traders. The time period for each brick can be as short as minutes or as long as a day, depending on current market conditions.

Renko charts are very useful for traders who prefer simple ways of spotting support and resistance levels as it focuses only on price movements. On the other hand, such specificity can make it more challenging to estimate general investor sentiment about a security.

Heikin Ashi

This type of chart traces its roots in Japan and is very comparable to candlestick trading charts in that the color of the body indicates a security's price movement for that period. This type of chart more clearly shows price trends through color-coding. When multiple green-colored candles follow each other with no lower shadows, the price is strongly trending upward. With continuous red-colored candles with no upper shadows or wicks, the price is strongly trending downward.

So, what is the difference between a candlestick price chart and a Heikin Ashi one? The latter charts or plots average price moves compared to actual prices for candlestick charts. By virtue of using average price moves, Heikin Ashi charts don't show exact opening and closing prices for a specific time frame.

Point and Figure Charts

This type of price chart is normally used by more sophisticated traders because it removes "noise" information by focusing only on meaningful price moves. A point-and-figure chart features columns of filtered price movements consisting of price boxes of O's and X's.

Time isn't considered when plotting point-and-figure charts. When there's no change in the chart, it means there's no change in the price of a security. Because point-and-figure price charts simplify drawing of trend, support and resistance lines, they're very ideal for identifying trends and trend reversals.

Chart Patterns

One of the ways technical analysis signals trend continuations and reversals is through price chart patterns. To simply the term, it refers to a discernable formation of price movements that traders can identify using curves or trendlines.

There are two general types of chart patterns: continuation and reversal patterns. As the names suggest, continuation patterns indicate that a currently ongoing trend will continue while reversal patterns indicate its reversal.

Trendlines

Trendlines help traders identify support and resistance levels and are drawn by connecting successive troughs and peaks, respectively. Successively higher peaks and troughs (upward angled trendlines) indicate an upward trending or bullish market. On the other hand, successively lower peaks and troughs (downward angled trendlines) indicate a downward trending or bearish market. When the trendlines are relatively flat, i.e., successive peaks and trough levels are roughly the same or they move back and forth within a specific range for a specific period of time, the market is a sideways moving one or is in consolidation mode, which is basically trendless.

Continuation Patterns

Continuation patterns indicate a disruption or a pause of an ongoing trend. As price patterns form, it can be very hard or impossible to know whether the current trend will reverse or continue. This requires paying very close attention on the trendlines drawn for continuation patterns, particularly when prices break above or below such lines.

One assumption about continuation patterns is that price movements within such patterns tend to become wilder the longer the pattern persists. As a result, traders also believe that price movements after breaking out of continuation patterns also tend to be larger.

The following are some of the most common continuation patterns in technical analysis:

A) Pennants: These are drawn with two trendlines that will ultimately cross paths because they're moving in different directions. One the resistance line's moving downward while the support line's moving upward. Often times, trading volumes go down while the pennant pattern forms and spikes the moment prices break out of the pattern.

B) Flags/Wedges: These are drawn using two parallel running trendlines that either slope upward, downward, or sideways. Generally speaking, upward sloping flags are common in bearish markets while downward sloping flags are more common in bullish ones. In most cases, trading volume goes down while the flag is being formed then increases when prices break out of the formation.

C) Triangles: Because this pattern appears more frequently than the others, it's one of the most popular technical analysis price chart patterns. There are three kinds of triangle patterns, all of which can last as long as several months:

A) Symmetrical triangles, with two trendlines approaching one another, which signals a likely price breakout but not its direction;

B) Ascending triangles, with a flat resistance line and an upward sloping support line that suggests a likely upward price breakout; and

C) Descending triangles, with a flat support line and downward sloping resistance line that suggests a likely price breakdown.

The height of the vertical line to the left of a triangle pattern suggests the magnitude of impending price breakout or breakdown.

D) Cups and Handles: This is a bullish (upward trending) continuation pattern. The cup-looking left part of the pattern resembles the shape of the letter U or a bowl, with both sides of said "cup" registering equal high prices. To the right of the "cup" is the handle, which is formed by a brief price pullback that looks more like a pennant or flag continuation pattern. After the handle is completed, the price of the security concerned will most likely breakout and reach new highs and continue its upward trend.

Reversal Patterns

As the name suggests, these are price chart patterns that signal the end of a trend and the start of a new one. This signals that one camp has run out of steam and the other camp has overcome them already until the beaten camp regains momentum and the winning camp eventually loses momentum and the trend is reversed.

Take for example a reversal in a previous bull market, where bullish traders outnumber and outpower bearish ones. When the bullish traders lose steam, the bears overpower them reverse the trend from a bullish to a bearish one, and continue to rule a market until they lose momentum themselves and the bulls regain it to reverse the trend again.

When reversals happen during market peaks, they're called distribution patterns. This indicates more traders are eager to sell than to buy, causing prices to reverse and start going down.

When reversals happen during market bottoms or troughs, they're called accumulation patterns. It's because more traders are eager to buy or accumulate more of a particular security, which starts to push the price up and reverse the bearish trend.

Much like continuation patterns, the size of the price breakout at reversal is highly influenced by the length of time reversal patters take to form. The longer it takes, the greater the price move upon breakout or reversal.

Some of the most common reversal price chart patterns include:

A) Head and Shoulders: This type of pattern appears as a series of three price pushes that include an initial peak (first shoulder), a second but higher peak (the head), and a third peak (second shoulder) that closely resembles the first one. A head and shoulders pattern occurs at the end of a bull market or trend, the completion of which signifies a reversal to a bearish market or trend.

B) Inverse Head and Shoulders: This pattern is formed by three major price movements as the head and shoulders, albeit in an opposite direction. It includes an initial trough (first inverted shoulder), a second but lower trough (the inverted head), and a third trough that approximates the first one (second inverted shoulder). This type of reversal pattern occurs towards the end of a bear market or trend, the completion of which signals a reversal to a bullish market or trend.

C) Double Tops and Bottoms: These patterns represent two attempts at breaking through established resistance and support levels. A double top pattern resembles the letter M, where the price unsuccessfully tries to breach a specific resistance level during a bull market or bullish trend. These unsuccessful attempts often lead to a reversal, i.e., a bear market or trend.

A double bottom pattern happens during bear markets and resembles the letter W where prices fail to breach a specific support level. Such unsuccessful attempts result in a trend reversal to a bull market.

D) Triple Tops: This reversal pattern resembles that of the double tops/bottoms but with an extra top/bottom. Compared to double tops/bottoms and head and shoulders patterns, triple tops are unicorns in that they don't happen frequently.

E) Price Gaps: As the name suggests, gaps are empty spaces that lie between two particular time periods. Gaps form when the next period's security price has jumped or dropped considerably from the previous period. For example, the price of Stock A closed at $5.00 the day before and opened at $6.00 the next trading day, resulting in a $1.00 gap.

There are three kinds of price gaps: breakaway, runaway, and exhaustion gaps. The difference between the three lies in their timing.

Breakaway gaps occur at the start of a new trend. Runaway gaps occur in the middle and exhaustion gaps occur towards the end of an existing trend.

Chapter 4

Technical Analysis:
Swing Charting

In essence, swing trading is all about price trends and momentum. As more and more traders make consistently superior trading profits using swing trading, it continues to grow in popularity among traders. And when it comes to technical analysis for swing trading, swing charts have become swing traders' weapons of choice. And in this chapter, we'll look at how to create and use swing charts for profitable swing trading.

Why Swing Charts Are Popular Among Swing Traders

One of the reasons for the increasing popularity of swing charts is simplicity. Swing charts, like any other form of technical analysis price charts, are all about looking for trends to take advantage of. All one needs to do is look at price charts. That's it!

Compared to other technical analysis tools, swing charts create much less "noise" or distortions. These refer to false triggers or signals that can result in taking unprofitable positions. Because there are less noise or distortions, the probabilities of being able to correctly identify trends and trade them profitably can be much higher than other forms of technical analysis.

The Bar Chart

Price bars are the primary building blocks of swing charts. Therefore, the foundation for creating a swing chart is a bar chart.

Each bar in a bar chart contains 4 important pieces of information: the open, high, low, and closing prices for the day, collectively known as OHLC. Some bar charts omit the open prices, using the high, low, and closing prices only (HLC). These help swing traders evaluate ongoing trends, identify possible trend reversals, and observe volatility in price swings.

A price bar consists of three lines:

A) The vertical line shows the highest and lowest prices for the day, with the top of the line being the highest and the bottom indicating the lowest price;

B) The left horizontal line represents the opening price; and

C) The right horizontal line represents the closing price.

Many traders color-code price charts for easier trend analysis. Many stock-trading platforms color price bars red when the closing price is lower than the opening price while price bars with closing prices higher than opening ones are usually colored green or black. And many of today's platforms provide many time period options for bar charts, from one minute, hour, day, week or month, the options are endless.

Creating a Swing Chart

Once traders have access to a bar chart, they can already create a swing chart. While most trading platforms can automatically generate this, learning how it's constructed can provide a much deeper insights on interpreting and acting upon swing chart developments to profit from swing trades.

When it comes to constructing swing charts, the most relevant pieces of information needed from bar charts are the high and low prices for each period. The most popular and seemingly most effective type of swing charting technique is the Gann technique. And from these pieces of information, one can identify four basic price turning points, i.e., trend reversals:

- Up Day: The highest and lowest prices for the period are higher than the immediately preceding one and is often colored green;

- Down Day: The highest and lowest prices for the period are lower than the immediately preceding one and is often colored red;

- Inside Day: The highest price for the period is lower and the lowest price is higher compared to the immediately preceding period and is often colored black; and

- Outside Day: The highest price for the period is higher and the lowest price for the period is lower than the immediately preceding period and is often colored blue.

Using the four turning points above, swing traders can identify the start and end of trends. To start generating swing charts, time is disregarded as a factor and price movements become the only relevant factor, which requires finding two important turning points:

A) A down day following an up day; and

B) An up day following a down day.

These two turning points tell traders when trends begin or end. As such, they're signals to take or close swing-trading positions. Once these two points have been identified, swing chart generating can commence.

As mentioned earlier, time is disregarded and only the price movements, particularly the two identified price turning points, are relevant. This means that all the price bars (sans the opening and closing prices) will be moved together using the same time intervals (day, week, etc.) and keeping the original sequence.

For example, an up day occurs 4 days before a down day. The three days in between will not be counted and only the up day and the down day will be connected. A typical swing chart would then look like this, which makes price trends much easier to see.

Swing Charting

Keeping the two price turning points in mind, swing charting involves taking or closing positions using such points as triggers or signals for doing so:

A) An up day following a down day turning point is a signal or trigger to buy a financial security; and

B) A down day following an up day turning point is a signal or trigger to sell a financial security.

That's how simple using a swing chart is. Traders can use swing charts for several purposes, such as:

A) Seeing the general trend of specific markets or financial securities in a very easy and practical way, sans the "distortions" or noises, and by just looking for turning points via the stairs-like patterns or trendlines.

B) Taking stop-loss or profit-taking positions via the turning points, i.e., previous selling and buying turning points can act as points of reference for future swing trades.

C) Using other advanced but not time-sensitive technical analysis tools like Elliott Waves and the Fibonacci technique, which are considered as leading technical indicators.

D) Creating price bands or channels, within which traders can set fairly reliable buying and profit-taking positions.

Swing charting can make it much easier for traders to identify price trends by removing the element of time and price "noise" from the equation. And because it can do so, it can also make it much easier and simpler to consistently make winning swing trades.

Chapter 5

Technical Analysis Indicators

Technical indicators refer to mathematical models that strive to predict a security or market's future price movements using data such as historical prices, trading volume, and open interest. Some of the most popular technical indicators traders use to time their trades include the moving averages (MA), moving average convergence divergence (MACD), relative strength indicator (RSI), Money Flow Index (MFI), Stochastics, and Bollinger Bands.

Types of Technical Indicators

Being a form of technical analysis, indicators focus on a security's historical trading data such as price, volume and open interest. There are two general types of technical indicators:

1. Oscillators: These indicators feature numbers that fluctuate between a specified minimum and maximum number, which are plotted below or above an existing price chart. The RSI, MACD and stochastic oscillator fall under this category.

2. These indicators are plotted on top of the actual prices on a security's price chart. MA and Bollinger Bands fall under this category.

Traders normally use multiple technical indicators when they time their trades. Given the myriad number of available technical indicators, traders need to choose and focus on a couple of indicators only and master them. The right indicators can result in trading riches while wrong ones can plunder any trader with huge trading losses. Because of their highly quantitative nature, they can be easily incorporated into any trading software or platform for easier use.

Many newbie traders make the mistake of choosing technical indicators based on what other, more seasoned traders use, even if they don't fully understand how such indicators work. Worse, many newbie traders try to use as many indicators as possible "just to make sure."

Don't make the same mistake when starting to use technical indicators for swing trading because this is one instance where the old saying "the more, the merrier" isn't applicable. The purpose of using technical analysis, which includes technical indicators, is to simplify the profitable trading process. Using too many technical indicators will make trading more complicated, especially when they give seemingly contradictory signals because they look at the market through different angles.

As you learned earlier from a previous chapter, technical indicators can also be lagging or leading. Lagging indicators identify trends that have already reversed or started. These include:

A) Trend indicators, which analyze the market or security's price trend, e.g., upward, downward or sideways;

B) Mean reversion indicators, which measure a price swing's magnitude before it retracts or pulls back; and

C) Volume indicators, which measure the number of buy-up (bullish) and sell-down (bearish) trades to estimate investors' general sentiment about a security.

On the other hand, leading indicators indicate a trend that's about to reverse or start. These indicators include:

A) Relative strength indicators, which measures buying and selling strength or pressure;

B) Momentum indicators, which measures the speed of price changes over time to measure a trend's momentum; and

C) Volume indicators.

Choosing and setting up technical indicators for profitable swing trading depends on a trader's trading style, which requires sufficient experience and skill. Given this, how can newbie swing traders choose the optimal technical indicators for them?

The best general approach is to start with using a couple of the most popular technical indicators first. There are reasons why they're the most popular, and one of them is many traders find them to be profitable trading tools. Over time, try to gauge whether they're working or if they need some tweaking.

Popular Technical Indicators for Newbie Traders

Exponential Moving Averages (EMA): 50 and 200 Days

Moving averages refer to the average prices of securities over a specific period of time, let's say the last 10 trading days. Because the average only considers the last X-number of trading days, the price population from which averages are computed change every day.

Let's say you're using a 10-day moving average. Let's say there are 22 trading days last month. On the 10th trading day, the ten-day average closing price is the average closing price from the first to the tenth trading day of last month. On the 11th trading day, the average closing price is that from the second to the eleventh trading day, and so on.

The reason it's called a moving average is because the population from which the average is computed moves or changes as time goes by. The last X number of days today will be different from that of tomorrow. This is called a simple moving average.

Exponential moving averages are different from simple ones in that the latest prices have more weight in computing the average compared to the oldest ones. The logic behind giving more premium to the most recent data is relevance; i.e., the market data becomes less relevant as time goes by.

How do traders use moving averages? They usually do it in pairs, a short-term moving average and a longer-term one. One of the most popular pairs traders use for exponential moving averages are the 50-day and the 200-day moving averages.

On an upward trending security, the short-term moving average will be above the long-term one by virtue of the latter using more prices from the past, which are lower. The moment that the short-term moving average crosses over and goes below the long-term moving average, it's a signal that the bullish trend has ended and a bearish one has already begun. This is a "sell" signal."

On a downward trending security, the short-term moving average will be lower than the long-term one. This is because longer moving averages trail shorter ones, which means it takes into consideration more prices from the past, which in this case are higher prices. The moment that short-term moving average cross above the long-term one for the period, it's a signal that the bearish trend has ended and a bullish one has begun already. This is a "buy" signal.

Bollinger Bands

Bollinger bands are technical indicators that use standard deviations to identify a band or price range in which a security's moving average is expected to oscillate or move. But how are Bollinger bands used in swing trading?

Traders who use this technical indicator believe that a security becomes more overbought when its price moves closer to the upper band and more oversold when it moves closer to the lower one. John Bollinger, the creator of this technical indicator, has 22 rules governing the trading use of his bands.

Another way traders use this indicator is through the "squeeze," i.e., the width of the band. Since the upper and lower bands represent upper and lower standard deviations of the price and it's a measure of volatility, the price of a security is deemed to become more volatile the wider the band becomes. The narrower it gets, the less volatile the price becomes.

With increased volatility comes the potential for greater price swings, which is what swing traders are looking for. Therefore, when the bands widen, it's a signal for swing traders to take positions because good swing trading opportunities are present. On the other hand, a narrowing band signals that it's time to close a position because less volatility means less meaningful price swings.

It's important to note the limitations of Bollinger bands to avoid using them erroneously. One of them is that Bollinger bands only indicate volatility and possible swing trading opportunities, not trend reversals. This leads us to the second limitation of Bollinger bands: they're not stand-alone trading systems. Even John Bollinger himself suggests that this indicator be used together with other indicators such as the relative strength index (RSI), moving averages, and on-balance volume.

Relative Strength Index

This is a technical indicator that measures a price movement's momentum through the size of recent price movements. It evaluates whether a particular security's price is already oversold or overbought.

The RSI's value ranges from 0 to 100 only, represented by a line graph that moves in between these two values. Traders interpret an RSI of above 70 as a security becoming overvalued already, i.e., overbought, which makes a trend reversal or price correction highly possible. An RSI of below 30 indicates that a security has become oversold or undervalued, which makes an upward reversal or correction in a downward trend highly likely.

Moving Average Convergence-Divergence (MACD)

MACD is a technical indicator that follows price trends by using two exponential moving averages (EMAs) for a security's price – the 12-period and 26-period EMAs.

The MACD for a particular trading day is computed by subtracting the 26-period EMA from the 12-period EMA. The resulting MACDs are plotted on the price chart and connected to create a MACD line.

Next, a 9-period EMA of the MACD, a.k.a., the signal line, is computed and plotted on top of or below the existing MACD line. The MACD line functions as a buying or selling trigger for traders. When the MACD line crosses to below the signal line, it's a signal for traders to take a short position on a security, i.e., to sell it. When the MACD line crosses above the signal line, it's a trigger for them to take a long position on a security, i.e., buy it.

When the 12-period EMA is higher than the 26-period one, the MACD's value is considered positive, which is usually colored blue in computer-plotted charts. When the 12-period EMA's lower than the 26-period EMA, the value's negative and is usually colored red. The farther the MACD is above or below the baseline, the greater the gap between the two EMAs is.

Often times, MACD is shown with a histogram that shows how wide the gaps are between the signal line and the MACD. The histogram is above the MACD baseline when the MACD is above the signal line and below the baseline if the MACD is below the signal line. Traders can estimate the strength of trend momentums through the MACD histogram.

Traders use the MACD indicator in a couple of ways. One is through crossovers. As mentioned earlier, traders sell their securities when the MACD crosses to below the 9-day EMA signal line. Conversely, traders take positions in or buy securities when the MACD crosses to above the signal line. But because the MACD isn't a perfect trading system, many traders wait to confirm such crossings over before taking or unloading positions in securities to minimize the risks of unprofitable trades.

MACD crossovers tend to be more accurate when they correspond to current prevailing trends. When the MACD crosses above the signal line after a short correction phase during a long-term bullish trend, they can be interpreted as confirmations of a bullish sentiment on securities. But when MACDs go below the signal line after a short spike during a long-term down trend, they can be interpreted as a confirmation of a bearish sentiment.

Another way traders use the MACD is through divergence. To be specific, divergence refers to when the MACD's highs or lows deviate from the related highs and lows of the security's price. When the security's MACD forms two increasing lows that correspond to two decreasing lows of a security's price, it's called a bullish divergence. This is considered by many traders as a valid bullish signal for a long-term bull market, which may be taken to mean as a position-taking signal for swing trading.

When the MACD creates two consecutive falling highs while the security's high prices go up for two consecutive periods, it's considered as a bearish divergence. When it appears during an ongoing bear market, it's interpreted as a confirmation that the bear market will most likely persist. Thus, it can be treated as a sign to either liquidate a position or wait further until taking a swing trading position on a security.

Quick falls and rises in the MACD can also indicate possible changes in buying or selling pressure or momentum of a security, i.e., an impending change in trend. In particular, sharp rises and falls can indicate overbought and oversold positions, both of which indicate possible reversal of a trend and opportunities to swing trade. In this regard, traders often use the MACD with the RSI or relative strength index.

While the MACD and RSI both indicate whether a security is overbought or oversold, they're different in one aspect. RSI price changes while MACD uses the difference between two exponential moving averages or EMAs. Because they both indicate whether a security is overbought or oversold using different parameters, traders often use them together for a more complete analysis of securities' buying or selling pressure.

MACD isn't a perfect indicator, too. One of the challenges of using MACD relates to divergence. In particular, it can produce trend reversal signals that don't result in actual reversals, which are also called as "false positives." Also, can also fail to identify actual reversals.

On-Balance Volume (OBV)

Trading volume can give traders insights on how the general investing public feels about a security, i.e., bearish or bullish, especially in conjunction with price chart patterns. Unusually high trading volume during significant price drops or spikes may confirm trend reversals or continuations, depending on the price action. Accumulation-distribution indicators help interpret market sentiment through trading volume with greater accuracy than simply looking at trading volume alone.

On-Balance Volume or OBV is a technical indicator developed during the 1960s, which totals up and down volumes and adds or subtracts their results continuously to create smoother volume indicating lines that are akin to price bars or charts. These lines make it easier to analyze volume trends together with price trends for more accurate swing trading signals.

OBV provides a highly accurate way of confirming major price peaks and troughs, which make them an ideal tool for estimating potential price spikes or drops. Using OBV is simple: just compare the OBVs movement to that of a security's prices, paying close attention to convergences or divergences between the two. The following are some of the ways the two interact, including what they mean:

A) The OBV reaching a new peak as the security's price tests an established resistance level indicates a bullish divergence. This signifies a high probability that the security's price will breach the established resistance level and surge upward.

B) The security's price reaching a new peak as its OBV tests an established resistance level indicates a bearish divergence. This signifies a high probability that an upward trend will either pause or reverse soon.

C) The OBV dropping to a new low as the security's price tests an established support level indicates a bearish divergence. This signifies a high probability that the security's price will breach the support and drop even further.

D) The security's price hitting a new low while its OBV tests an established support level indicates a bullish divergence. It signifies that the security price's downtrend may either pause or reverse soon.

On Choosing Technical Indicators

Choosing technical indicators to use, especially as a newbie swing trader, can be overwhelming. Fortunately, it's something that can be done well by choosing any or all of the above-mentioned popular technical indicators. They're some of the most popular for very good reasons, some of which include practicality and accuracy.

Chapter 6

Preparing Your Mind
for Swing Trading Success

Even the most sensible swing trading strategies can fail without the right mindsets. This is because wrong mindsets often lead to wrong decisions, which include not following the swing trading strategy chosen or worse, not choosing one at all and just "winging" it. In this chapter, we'll take a look at some of the best ways to develop a profitable swing trading mindset.

Flexibility

The bamboo is one of the strongest trees around, being able to withstand the strongest of storms despite its seeming frail structure. How's it able to do that?

By being the most flexible of all trees. When it is hit by the strongest winds one can imagine, it simply bends in the direction of such winds. Instead of resisting the inevitable, they adapt to it. Other bigger and stronger trees that aren't as flexible get uprooted while the bamboo remains where it is.

By flexibility, a swing trader must:

A) Not get attached to any of his or her trades;

B) Be able to change opinions and strategies when situations call for it because swing trading isn't about being "right" or firm but about making money.

C) Accept reality instead of always trying to "bend" it. No swing trader can control the market but can only surf its waves to profitability or get wiped out by trying to oppose it.

Value the Importance of Proper Execution

Implementing swing trading strategies properly can substantially increase the chances of profitable swing trades. Improper or worse, non-implementation of chosen strategies increase one's chances of losing trades. In fact, it can guarantee losing trades.

When it comes to proper execution of swing trading strategies, the following are important things to prioritize:

A) Choosing the most appropriate tools and strategies for profitable swing trades.

B) Set demarcation lines and stick to them. Not all trades will be profitable, but losses can be minimized by setting stop-loss and profit-taking limits. Without such limits, swing trading losses can grow beyond reasonable limits and profits that could've already been earned may be wiped out if held on for too long waiting for prices to go up indefinitely.

C) Consistently executing strategies.

D) Taking reasonable and well-calculated risks.

Use Numbers to Trade, Not Feelings

I remember over ten years ago when I let my emotions rule my swing trading. I bought shares of stock of a prominent real estate company and within 2 months of holding it, I already had a paper gain of about 30%.

However, I felt really good about earning a 30% ROI in just 2 months and was very optimistic that I could double my money if I held on to my position for another couple of months. When its price dropped and reduced my ROI to only 15%, I justified it by saying "It's just a correction." When the ROI became negative 10%, I still repeated the same mantra. Eventually I cut my losses at 25%.

My optimism turned out to be nothing more than greed. Had I established a profit-taking point and stuck to it regardless, I would've locked in on my profits instead of losing money on that swing trade.

By setting limits both ways, i.e., profit-taking or stop-loss limits, you can minimize your swing trading risks because you rely on something objective and unchanging, unlike emotions.

Speaking of numbers, part of relying on numbers when swing trading is to focus on overall swing trading results instead of individual trades. Why?

No trader is perfect and there will always be losing trades. When you focus on individual trades, you can get discouraged. But when you look at it from a wider, general perspective, you can more accurately evaluate your swing trading results.

For example, only three of your 10 swing trades two years ago made money but overall, you accomplished an ROI of 50% for that year because those three winning trades made lots of profits while the losses of the seven other trades weren't big.

The following year, six of your 8 swing trades were profitable and only two were losing trades. However, the losses on those two trades were so huge that you ended the year with an ROI of negative 10%.

Between the two years, which was better: the first year when only 30% of your trades were profitable, but you ended the year with an overall return of 50% (focus on overall trading results) or the second year when 75% of your trades were profitable (focus on individual trades), but you lost money overall? I bet you'll say you that the first year was better – and you'd be right!

Learn from Your Mistakes Instead of Being Discouraged by Them

If everybody makes mistakes, why should you think you're an exemption and beat yourself up over them? Consider Thomas Edison on successfully inventing the light bulb that forever changed human history for the better. He failed a thousand times before finally getting the working version of the light bulb right. When interviewed by a newspaper publication on how he handled those 1,000 failed experiments, he answered that those weren't failures but were simply 1,000 lessons on how not to make a working lightbulb. He didn't get discouraged by his mistakes because he knew that mistakes are valuable lessons on what not to do the next time.

When it comes to swing trading, nobody has a batting average of 100% - even computer programs. It's because price movements aren't governed by fixed laws of science but by finicky laws of human psychology. You only have to choices when you make mistakes: learn from them or quit because of them. It's up to you.

Successful swing traders remain unperturbed by losing trades but instead, they persist wisely by learning from their mistakes.

Find and Stick to Trading Strategies That Work for You

While starting with the most popular trading strategies is a good place to start swing trading, you must come evaluate the results you get from your chosen strategy to see if it's worth continuing, tweaking or replacing.

What do you need to consider when evaluating whether a trading strategy is something that you should stick to, tweak, or ditch? One is risk appetite. If your risk appetite is on the low side, maybe you shouldn't even be trading at all. If it's moderate, your trading strategy must be one that carries a moderate amount of risk, too.

Your swing trading time frame is another consideration. If you want to earn big returns in a few days or weeks, then you must be ready to take on higher risks as only highly volatile securities can give you opportunities to do so. If your risk tolerance is low to moderate, considering swing trading securities that aren't very volatile, albeit you'll need to extend your swing trading time frame to a few weeks or even a couple of months.

If you swing trade on a part time basis only, it means you can't dedicate as much time for it as those who do it full time. That being said, it'd be better if you choose to swing trade securities that aren't very volatile. Very volatile, but potentially very profitable, securities require closer monitoring for optimal trading results. Taking a swing trading position in a security that's very volatile and checking out its price once or twice a day only can put you at risk of either missing out on a potential bottom price for buying or a potential high price for selling. Worse, you may miss the security's profitable price level and end up with a losing swing trade when its price drops by the time you check it out again.

Always Be Learning

Financial markets today are more complex and rapid today than ever before. If you're not always learning new things or if you're not keeping up to date with financial markets and the economy in general, you may run the risk of reading your chosen markets wrong and end up with more losing swing trades than profitable ones.

Plan Your Swing Trades

As cliché as it may sound, failing to plan is indeed planning to fail. The worst swing trading strategy in the history of trader-kind is the wing-it strategy. Many traders make the mistake of just following the herd with nary a clue of why they're adopting the strategies of the trading herd and what the risk-reward tradeoffs of such strategies.

The following are some of the most important things you must consider when planning your swing trades:

A) Your target profit or rate of return on the trade;

B) Your stop-loss price level at which you'll liquidate your swing trades to cut losses;

C) How much money you're comfortable losing on your swing trades, especially when you're just starting out;

D) Will you need the money you're trading at some point and if so, when do you need it back;

E) Your swing trading time frame; and

F) Can you afford to hold your position for a much longer period of time in case the price of the security you're holding is still underwater after several months?

Remember, the more detailed your plan, the lesser the tendency that you'll rely on your emotions and "gut" feel to execute your trades, which will greatly increase your chances of executing profitable swing trades.

Practice a Lot before Trading Actual Dollars

While practice doesn't make perfect, it does lead to excellence. And when it comes to swing trading, excellence means a generally profitable collection of swing trades every year.

"But I don't have that much money to waste on practicing!" you might protest. Don't worry because practicing your swing trades, in the beginning, doesn't mean you'll have to stake real money.

You can practice what I refer to as "paper" swing trading. This means taking hypothetical positions using real time market prices of financial securities. Let's consider paper trading shares of Apple, Inc.'s stocks.

Let's say that using technical analysis, you reckon now is a good time to take a swing trading position in Apple's stocks. On a spreadsheet like Excel or Numbers, input the number of shares you hypothetically bought (let's say 100 shares) at the actual closing price of Apple stocks today, which we'll assume to be $100 per share. Your hypothetical investment in that position would be $10,000.

For the next few days or weeks, monitor the daily closing price of Apple shares until it either reaches your designated profit-taking price or drops to or below your chosen stop-loss price. When that happens, "liquidate" or "sell" your hypothetical shares to close your position and complete your swing trade.

Through paper trading, you can get a very good feel of how to choose financial securities to swing trade and when to trade them without having to burn through your precious money. Only when you feel you've had enough paper swing trades and feel comfortable risking your own money already should you swing trade for real.

Don't Think Too Highly of Yourself

Pride usually comes before the fall. It's no different with swing trading. Especially during bull markets, successive and hugely profitable swing trades tend to easily outnumber losing ones, which can get into traders' heads and make them feel invincible. When they feel that way, they no longer tend to question or evaluate themselves, which increases their risks for making cocky and stupid trades.

Don't be one of them. Regardless of how many successive profitable swing trades you make, continue making it habit to evaluate your trading strategies and yourself and look for areas for improvement. As long as you live and as long as you trade, there will always be room for improvement.

And when you make even small improvements to yourself and your trading strategies on a regular basis, you become a better and more profitable trader. And you make more money.

Chapter 7

Important Tips for Maintaining Swing Trading Momentum

As we end this book, I'd like to share with you a few important tips to maintain your swing trading momentum later on.

One of the things you'll need to remember about swing trading momentum is that managing it well is more of a fine art than an exact science. To successfully manage your swing trading momentum, you'll need to learn how to manage your trading risks wisely, to be a very patient person, and master your emotions. Compared to day trading where all your positions are closed within a few trading hours, swing trading takes days, weeks, and even a couple of months to come full circle. Its longer time frame requires a different trading viewpoint.

The following are four important things you should do to maximize your swing trading momentum and consequently, profits.

Set and Forget

As mentioned earlier, you'll need a lot of patience to succeed at swing trading. You shouldn't be monitoring every price tick that happens all throughout the trading day. Once you take a long position, forget it. Just take a look at its price once a day or every other day. With swing trades, you'll need to let your chosen securities build their momentum so you can enjoy potentially high profits.

If you micro-monitor your swing trading positions, you'll put yourself in a position where you'll be strongly tempted to liquidate earlier than you need to. When you succumb to such temptations, you'll either minimize your trading profits or maximize your losses because you prematurely liquidated your position.

So, just set price alerts near your primary profit-taking and stop-loss target prices and forget it. Just take action when the alerts are triggered.

Ditch the Micro Time Frames

With swing trading, you must focus more on the longer time frames because they're less volatile and by doing so, you minimize your risks for "false triggers" or whiplashes that can make you take positions on securities whose prices are still on a decline. The shortest time frame you should consider is daily, nothing less. The longer your time frame, the lesser the false triggers and noise you'll encounter, and the more you can maintain your winning swing trading streak.

Moving Averages for Risk Management

The easiest and most objective way to see a security's true trend is through moving averages. As such, moving averages can be your best ally in managing your swing trading risks and find more profitable swing trading entry points.

Often times, financial securities that are enjoying momentum retreat to their moving averages, the most common of which are the 20 and 50-day moving averages, before proceeding with the next price movement. As such, moving averages can help you time your swing trades with fairly high accuracy and ease.

Don't Cash in on Your Profits in One Fell Swoop

Many financial securities that are on a strong price momentum can continue for weeks and months on end. But the challenge is it's impossible to predict exactly how long bullish momentums run for specific securities. There's always the risk of liquidating too early when a security's price continues to soar after closing a position and waiting too long that its price has fallen deep from its peak.

By taking partial profits or liquidating part of your swing trading positions on securities that are on a strong upward momentum, you can lock in on some of the profits once your chosen security has reached your target profit-taking level. Because there are still some left, you can lock in on more profits if the momentum continues. If the price happens to come down after that, your initial profits could compensate for the smaller profit or loss on the remaining position.

Conclusion

Thank you for buying this book. I hope that through it, you were able to understand what Swing Trading is all about and more importantly, how to do it.

But knowing is only half the battle. The other half is action or application of knowledge. To make the most of what you learned and make it impact your life, you must apply the things you learned about swing trading in this book. Otherwise, everything you've read here is just for entertainment.

You don't have to apply everything at once. Start with one or two lessons for the next few days. Then apply another one or two for another few days and so on until you're able to apply what you learned and profit from swing trading.

So, what are you waiting for? Here's to your Swing Trading success my friend! Cheers!

Finally, if you enjoyed this book, then I'd like to ask you for a favor, would you be kind enough to leave a review for this book on Amazon? It'd be greatly appreciated!

Thank you and good luck!

References

https://bullsonwallstreet.com/4-rules-swing-trading-momentum/

https://eminimind.com/10-steps-to-developing-a-winning-traders-mindset-transcript/

https://www.investarindia.com/blog/technical-analysis-charts/

https://www.investopedia.com/articles/technical/112601.asp

https://www.investopedia.com/ask/answers/what-are-leading-lagging-and-coincident-indicators/

https://www.investopedia.com/terms/b/barchart.asp

https://www.investopedia.com/terms/b/bollingerbands.asp

https://www.investopedia.com/terms/m/macd.asp

https://www.investopedia.com/terms/r/rsi.asp

https://www.investopedia.com/terms/s/swingtrading.asp

https://www.investopedia.com/terms/t/technicalindicator.asp

https://www.investopedia.com/trading/introduction-to-swing-trading/

SWING TRADING

Best Techniques and Principles to Execute Swing Trading Strategies

WILLIAM RILEY

Introduction

You've probably heard about swing trading, especially stories of how many people have already made good money from doing it from home or anywhere with a good Internet connection and without having to slave away for hours on end. You may have also been familiar with the basics of swing trading but would like to learn strategies and techniques that'll help you become a successful swing trader and, hopefully, quit your boring corporate job.

In this book, I'll teach you principles and techniques that you can use to swing trade successfully. By the end of this book, you can start implementing these principles and strategies so that you can start your journey toward becoming a master swing trader.

So, if you're ready, turn the page and let's begin!

Chapter 1

Fundamental Analysis

Fundamental analysis refers to a method of analyzing financial securities, like stocks, and which involves studying their fundamentals, i.e., the basic financial information that helps determine their prices or values. For stocks, fundamentals include financial data in a company's statements of condition, profit and loss statements and cash-flow statements, statements of changes in equity, and business developments or events. For foreign currencies or Forex, fundamentals include economic data of the forex pair countries that influence exchange rates such as interest rates, trade balance, economic growth (GDP), inflation, and political events.

Fundamental analysis helps you answer the question of what financial securities to swing trade.

When looking at fundamentals, it's important to remember that fundamental financial data isn't very useful on a stand-alone basis. What this means is a single piece of data or information, such as net income or revenues for a single time period, won't tell you much other than if it made a profit or if it lost money, in this example. It doesn't tell you how profitable the company is or how efficient is it in terms of generating revenue using its existing asset base.

For example, let's say Company A reported a net income of $3.00 million dollars for the year 2018. If you just consider this single piece of information, what can you conclude about the company other than it was profitable for that year? Nothing. You won't be able to conclude how profitable it is, whether it can sustain its profitability, how efficient it was in using its assets to generate revenues, or if it's worth buying the stocks of Company A at the prevailing market price.

For this reason, there are three ways to conduct fundamental analysis: horizontal, vertical, and both. Allow me to explain the three in greater detail.

Horizontal and Vertical Analysis

Horizontal analysis, i.e., time-series analysis refers to a comparison of data or information for different time periods. A good principle for conducting horizontal analysis is using at least four (4) time periods, which is the minimum for establishing a trend for at least three years, with the first year acting as the base year for comparative purposes.

Going back to our example earlier of Company A's 2018 net income of $3.00 million, what if its net income in the three years prior were $1.00 million in 2015, $1.5 million in 2016, and $2.25 million in 2017. Comparing 2018's net income to the previous three years, you will not just be able to conclude that the company is profitable. You'll also be able to conclude that it's becoming even more profitable in terms of net income.

Now, what if the net incomes for 2015, 2016 and 2017 were $6.00, $5.00 million and $3.50 million, respectively? Based on these two prior years, you'll see that its net income has plunged significantly, right? Therefore, while you can conclude that Company A is still profitable, you may have reasonable basis to believe that it may start losing money this year or next year.

Can you see the additional important insights you can glean through horizontal analysis of the same financial information, which can significantly help you to make much wiser stock-picking decisions?

Vertical analysis, i.e., ratio analysis, refers to comparing one piece of financial information in a company's financial statement to another one within the same time period. The reason it's called "vertical" is because being in the same time period, these pieces of information are arranged vertically along the same time period column, which is how accounts are presented in financial statements.

Vertical analysis gives you the ability to take a piece of financial information in better context or helps you make sense of something that doesn't on a stand-alone basis. Take for example, net income.

In our example earlier, Company A's net income for 2018 was $3.00 million. What if its total shareholders' equity, i.e., capital, was $5.00 million? It means that in 2018, Company A's return on investment or capital was:

$3.00 million ÷ $5.00 million = 60% Return on Investment

I don't know about you, but a 60% return on equity investment for one year is a whole lot! Not only can you conclude that Company A was profitable in 2018 but it was very, very profitable!

Now, let's say that instead of $5.00 million in total shareholder equity, Company A had $50 million. Given its $3 million net income for 2018, its return on equity investment or capital would then be:

$3 million ÷ $50 million = 6% Return on Investment

Now, 6% may not necessarily be a good annual return on investment compared to other companies. Through vertical analysis, you were able to see how profitable Company A is aside from it just being "profitable".

The best form of fundamental analysis involves combining the two, i.e., vertical + horizontal analysis. This means computing financial ratios for different time frames, at least three, and comparing them.

This gives you a much deeper insight on a company's financial condition and performance compared to just looking at a specific piece of financial information or ratio for a specific time frame.

Again, let's consider Company A's hypothetical $3 million dollars net income in 2018. Let's say that its return on equity investment (ROE or ROI), was 8% for that year. It gives you an idea of how profitable it may be to invest in Company A based on 2018 results.

However, what if its ROE for 2015, 2016 and 2017 were 13%, 12% and 10%, respectively? What would you conclude about its profitability for this year and possibly, even for the next few years? You'll see that from 2015, its ROE has dropped 5% over the last three years. It means that something's going on that continues to make the company less profitable, e.g., expenses growing faster than revenues, revenues slowing down, etc. With expectations of dwindling profitability, would you still consider investing in Company A? Would you have reason to believe that its stock price will go up considerably soon?

By the way, horizontal analysis also involves comparing a company's figures and ratios with its peers, i.e., competitors or similar companies in the same industry. Doing this can help you figure out how well, or poorly, managed a company is vis-a-vis other similar companies.

Fundamental Analysis and Swing Trading

Fundamental analysis can involve many different ratios and pieces of financial information. Considering swing trading involves a much shorter position than long-term, i.e., buy-and-hold, investors, you won't have to sift through all types of financial information and ratios just to pick the best stocks for swing trading. You'll just need to focus on those that have an impact on a stock's market value, which in most cases are profitability-related measures.

If you recall from earlier, swing trading involves looking for stocks – or other financial securities – that are currently undervalued and have a good potential to make a substantial price swing in the next few trading days, weeks, or at most, a couple of months. It doesn't look at long-term profits, i.e., over several years. But compared to day trading, it has a much longer time frame.

When it comes to fundamental analysis, the following are some of the relevant pieces of information you'll need to consider:

1. Net income;

2. Earnings-per-Share (EPS);

3. Price-to-Earnings Ratio (P/E Ratio);

4. ROE or ROI; and

5. Company and economic news that may have a significant impact on a company's profitability such as interest rates, foreign exchange rates, new industry regulations, etc.

Sources of Information and Financial Reports Needed

The United States' Securities and Exchange Commission (SEC) compels all companies whose publicly-issued financial instruments like stocks and bonds to make their audited financial statements available to the investing public. This means that as an investor, you can ask these companies for copies of their audited financial statements, which includes an annually-filed report called the 10K and a prospectus. These financial statements and reports include important items for fundamental analysis such as cash flows, balance sheet items, and other sorts of financial information.

And more than just "numbers", these also include important non-financial information that affect a company's profitability and going concern, i.e., longevity. These include information about the company's board of directors, management team, its competitors, its business plans and how economic developments may affect the company's operations, among others.

These reports are available in the companies' websites or you can simply Google "10K" or 'Prospectus" to get them via other reputable websites. One of the most reliable places where you can get audited financial statements, prospectuses, and 10Ks is Yahoo! Finance, which has these statements and reports for all companies that are publicly-listed in exchanges in the United States.

Another important report you'll need to consider when conducting fundamental analysis is the 8K, which is released once in a while. The information contained in the 8K is pretty much similar to the 10K. However, companies release 8Ks only when they have to release short-term but significant financial information to their investors. In some situations, the information companies disclose through 8K reports substantially impact their share's prices.

The Financial Statements

The three most important financial statements for fundamental analysis are the income statement (profit and loss statement), the balance sheet (statement of condition), and the cash flow statement.

As you may have gleaned from the name, income statements include financial information pertaining to a company's income such as:

1. Operating revenues, e.g., sales, fees, etc.;

2. Gross profit;

3. Operating expenses; and

4. Non-recurring revenues and expenses.

These pieces of information can help you determine a company's financial performance past and current performance. Your evaluation of past and current financial performance can help you make meaningful and reasonable expectations of future financial performance, which in the long run affects a company's financial condition and going concern (longevity).

As a swing trader, your primary concern is whether a company's stock has a good chance of exhibiting a significant price swing either way so you can earn substantial profits in the short term. Profitability is often the primary driver of share prices, which you can observe every time publicly-traded companies release earnings results. That's why you'll need to be very familiar with interpreting income statements.

The Balance Sheet, also called the Statement of Condition, shows a company's assets, liabilities, and net worth. Balance sheet accounts can be classified into several general categories:

1. Current Assets: These refer to the company's assets that are expected to be liquidated or converted back to cash within the next 12 months like accounts receivables from customers or highly marketable securities, i.e., financial securities that can be sold in financial markets at any time like shares of stocks of publicly-traded companies like Apple, Inc. or Facebook.

2. Non-Current Assets: Assets that aren't expected to be converted into cash within the next 12 months. These include long-term investments in thing like factories, properties, and equipment used for operations.

3. Current Liabilities: These refer to a company's financial obligations or debts that will have to be settled or paid within the next 12 months. These include salaries to employees that are already due but not yet paid, amount owed to suppliers for unpaid inventories, and utility bills like electricity.

4. Non-Current Liabilities: These refer to a company's financial obligations that can be paid after 12 months from the balance

sheet's date. These include bonds that the company has issued that aren't due to mature within 12 months or long-term bank debts.

5. Shareholders' Equity: This refers to the amount of capital infused by shareholders and previous years' earnings that were kept for future business plans like expansion or early retirement of debts. This amount represents how much the company is really worth, i.e., the difference between the value of its assets and its liabilities. When shareholders' equity is negative, i.e., the value of liabilities exceed the value of assets, a company is technically considered as bankrupt.

The Cash Flow Statement gives you a summary of the accounts that have impacted a company's cash balances for a specific period of time. These include:

1. Net Income;

2. Changes in Inventories;

3. Changes in Liabilities;

4. Financing Opportunities;

5. Depreciation Expenses; and

6. Other Cash Transactions.

Cash flows can provide very good insights on a company's financial health and performance, which in turn affects its longevity. In particular, inventory turnover, i.e., magnitude of changes or movements in inventory levels, can give you a very good idea of how well the company's sales are going.

Time Frame

When it comes to swing trading, you'll need to focus more on quarterly data compared to annual data. Why? It's because swing trading is more concerned with short-term price movements. Quarterly data allows you to make more accurate evaluations because quarterly data has a greater impact on short-term price swings than long-term data, i.e., annual.

So, when you're evaluating quarterly financial data of companies for shortlisting your swing trading candidates. In particular, you'll need to compare four other quarters, beginning with the same quarter the previous year. So, you'll be comparing the previous quarter with the 2nd, third, and fourth previous quarter plus the same quarter last year.

Why do you need to compare the last quarter's data with the same quarter last year? Doing so can help you make more accurate comparisons based on annual cycles or seasons.

Take for example a company that manufactures snow sports equipment. Chances are, it sells more of its products during or toward the winter season. So simply comparing its summer quarter sales to its winter or fall quarter sales won't be comparing apples to apples. By comparing sales figures, for example, for the winter quarter this year with that of last year, you can get a better estimate of this company's sales performance under similar conditions, which in this case is the winter or pre-winter season.

Earnings Calls

Every quarter, swing traders excitedly wait for one of the most important swing trading events, i.e., the quarterly earnings calls of publicly-listed companies. An earnings call is when publicly-traded companies publicly announce the results of their operations for the quarter, i.e., revenues, income, etc.

Because earnings or profitability is considered to be the primary driver of share prices, earnings calls can have significant impact on a stock price's short-term movements or swings. The more dramatic the reported results are, the more dramatic a stock's price swing in the near-term can be, which means very good swing-trading opportunities. On the other hand, mundane or mediocre reported results have minimal or no impact on a stock price's near-term price swing, which means little or no swing trading opportunities.

For example, if Company A's projected net income growth for the quarter was 10% but its earnings call for that quarter reported a growth of only 5%, chances are high that investors will react negatively to the "shortfall". And by reacting negatively, I mean there'll probably be a short-term sell-off of Company A's stock, which means a downward price swing in the near term.

On the other hand, when Company A's reported net income growth for the previous quarter was 15% and the projected was only 10%, guess how investors will probably respond? That's right, positively. This means that more likely than not, the price of Company A's stock will most likely register an upward swing in the near term.

Regardless of how the price can swing in the short term, you as a swing trader can take advantage and earn a nice profit. If the earnings call results are very positive, you can take a long position and close it once the upward swing reaches your target price or when it seems to have already lost steam. If the earnings call results are negative, you can still profit by taking a short position and close it later on when the stock's price has dropped to your target level.

The thing with earnings calls is that it's impossible to determine – in advance – how they'll go. You won't be able to perfectly predict the information that scheduled earnings calls will divulge. However, what's more important is knowing how the market often reacts to a company's earnings calls. And this is something that you can reasonably expect to learn to do.

How? You can do this by simply going over a company's previous earnings calls and comparing how its share prices swung based on the content of those calls. This can help you get a reasonable estimate of how the market may react to a company's upcoming earnings call, which can help you swiftly take positions as soon as results of an earnings call goes out.

For example, you must be ready to enter a position, long or short, shortly before a company conducts its earnings call. This means determining beforehand how many shares and how much of a position you'll take. That way, you can almost immediately take a position after the quarterly results are announced and beat majority of the market to a profitable swing trading position. If you wait too long, you may miss the ideal position entry price and fail to execute a profitable enough swing-trade.

Important Ratios to Consider

As mentioned earlier, vertical analysis or ratio analysis helps you process financial information presented in a company's financial statements and make more accurate assessments of a company's financial health and performance, both of which increase your chances of executing a profitable swing trade on company's stock. For swing trading purposes, you don't need to compute or look at all financial ratios. You'll only need to focus on a few important ones that may have a substantial impact on a stock price's potential swing.

Price-Earnings (P/E) Ratio

This ratio gives you an idea of how cheap or expensive a stock's price is in relation to its current earnings per share (EPS). In case you're not yet familiar with the EPS, it's computed by dividing a company's net income for a specific period of time over the total number of outstanding shares as of cut-off date.

For example, Company A's net income for 2018 was $3.00 million while outstanding number of shares as of end of 2018 was 6.00 million shares. The EPS would be:

$3.00 million ÷ 6.00 million shares = $0.50 Per Share

This means that Company A's EPS for 2018, the amount of money each share of stock earned that year, was $0.50 or 50 cents per share.

Going back to the P/E ratio, this is computed by dividing a stock's current market price by its EPS. If Company A's stock closed at $5.00 today and its latest EPS was $0.50/share, then its P/E ratio would be:

$5.00 ÷ $0.50 = 10 Times Earnings

This metric is expressed as "times earnings" because it represents how much investors are currently willing to pay for each share of stock's earnings. In the example above, the P/E ratio of 10 times means that as of the moment, investors are willing to pay 10 times its EPS for the opportunity to earn $0.50 per share of Company A's stock.

The P/E ratio tells you how cheap or expensive a share of stock is. The higher the value, the more expensive it is and vice-versa. So, if you compare Company A's P/E ratio of 10 times to a P/E ratio of 20 times for a similar or competitor company, Company A's stock is the "cheaper" stock and thus, is the better buy for purposes of swing trading.

One thing you should consider about evaluating P/E ratios is that you must never take it at face value for in and by itself, it really holds no value. The proper way to use P/E ratios is to compare them to P/E ratios of other stocks within the same industry, with the industry's average P/E ratio, and the market's average P/E ratio. Doing so gives it context by which you can make wise swing trading decisions.

The idea of "cheap" or "overvalued" is often hinged on the context of the value of other similar assets. The only reason we can say that the iPhone is expensive is because there are a myriad number of similar products, i.e., smartphones, that sell for much less. If the iPhone is the only smartphone brand in the world, how can we objectively say it's cheap or expensive other than based on our ability to afford it?

Now, what do you make of stocks that have high P/E ratios relative to other similar companies and its industry? This can mean either:

1. Its stock price may be due for a price correction at some point in the future; or

2. The company has done or achieved something that has made many investors believe that its current price level is reasonable and can result in substantial returns in the future.

When this happens, consider looking at the company's financial statements and reports and compare it with its competitors. You may also want to check out recent news about the company in the papers or financial websites like Yahoo! Finance, Bloomberg, or Reuters. These can give you a reasonable basis for concluding if the stock price is due for a correction or if the stock is worth buying still at its high P/E ratio.

Generally speaking, if a company's P/E ratio appears to be excessively high or low vis-a-vis its competitors' and its industry's, it may indicate a possible price correction, a.k.a., price swing, in the coming days, weeks, or months.

If its P/E ratio is excessively high, it means that the stock may already be overvalued and as a result, it's highly possible that its prices may drop soon to a level that's more appropriate or justifiable for its industry or niche. This may be a good opportunity to take a short swing trading position.

On the other hand, if a stock's P/E ratio is excessively low despite the company's very good financials, this may indicate that its stock is very much undervalued and that it's currently selling at a bargain. As such, it may be due for an upward price correction or swing to better approximate its competitors' and industry's P/E ratio. This may be a very good opportunity to take a long swing trading position.

Another important thing to consider about P/E ratios is that there's no right or wrong number. It's always relative to others in the same industry or niche and to some extent, to the P/E ratio of the entire market. It's a bad idea to automatically consider a P/E ratio of 10 times as "cheap" or a buy signal if other similar companies' P/E ratios are less than 10 times. Consequently, you can't say that a stock with P/E ratio of 20 times is expensive if others in its industry or niche have an average P/E ratio of 30 times.

It's worth noting that a company's and its industry's age can result in higher or lower average P/E ratios. Young companies that belong to relatively young industries with still very high growth potential like Facebook and Google have higher average P/E ratios compared to older and more established companies in older, more established industries like JP Morgan Chase and Citigroup. Why?

Young companies in fast growing sectors have a high probability of increasing their future EPS by huge amounts over the years. That means there's a high possibility that today's current market price will be very low compared to its future EPS and as EPS grows, so will market price.

On the other hand, income of companies in more established and steady but low-growth industries like banking aren't expected to grow as fast as they used to during their younger years. Hence, older and more established companies, i.e., blue-chip stocks, generally have lower average P/E ratios.

Finally, the P/E ratio shouldn't be the sole basis for taking swing trading positions. However, it's a very good starting point or filter for short-listing good stocks for swing trading.

Chapter 2

Technical Analysis

As mentioned earlier, fundamental analysis helps you choose which financial securities, e.g., stocks, to swing trade. Technical analysis, on the other hand, helps you answer the question of when to execute your swing trades.

Technical analysis is, simply put, analyzing a security's price movements to determine the timing of one's position taking and closing. In short, technical analysis seeks to answer the questions:

1. When should you take a long (buy) or short (position)?

2. When should you close your open position?

Financial Information Needed

Take note that with technical analysis, you don't need a lot of financial or economic information. All you need to analyze is the historical market prices and trading volumes of financial securities. Those are the only things you need, nothing more, nothing less.

Why is that so? One of the principles underlying technical analysis is that assumption that all possible information that can be discovered about a financial security is already factored into its current market price. That being said, one needs to concern him or herself only with the price movements, which is believed to be more than enough to evaluate investors' general sentiments or beliefs about where the price of a security will go in the future.

Volume is required because it gives traders an idea of the strength of price swings. Trading volume is a very good indicator of demand – or lack thereof – for a particular financial security. The higher the trading volume compared to the average, the greater the demand and the stronger the support for a price swing.

For example, if Company A's stock price goes up by 10% in one day but its trading volume is 10% less than its average daily trading volume, it's highly unlikely that the upward trend will continue. It's because lower than average trading volume indicates lack of interest or support.

On the other hand, if Company A's stock price goes up by 5% in one day and that day's trading volume was twice its daily average, there's clearly a great deal of interest and support for that price movement. This may indicate a high probability that the upward price swing will continue.

Analysis Tools

Technical analysis relies on two types of tools: price charts and technical indicators. Price charts are visual representations of a financial security's price movement. A quick look at a price chart will be enough to tell you a security's current price trend, i.e., bullish (upward), bearish (downward), or sideways (consolidation).

There are different kinds of price charts but the most popular price chart traders use, whether day traders or swing traders, is the Japanese candlestick. We'll talk more about this later on but suffice to say, this type of price chart shows a security's opening, closing, highest, and lowest prices for a particular time period. Normally, it also depicts trading volume at the bottom of the chart.

Technical indicators are metrics that attempt to measure the strength of a particular price swing or movement. When a price swing or movement has been shown to have lost momentum, a price movement or trend reversal may be on the horizon. By telling traders like you when a current price movement is already losing momentum, it can help you time your trades such that you optimize your chances of executing profitable swing trades.

Price Charts

This refers to a much simpler and visuals-oriented way of conducting technical analysis. As mentioned earlier, it simply involves plotting the price movements of securities via charts. And by merely looking at these charts, you can already glean ideas of a particular security's price trend.

While looking at price charts can help you identify a security's current trend, you will still need to do other things aside from just looking to time your trades well. In particular, you'll need to identify two important price levels: support and resistance.

The support level is where a security's market price often bounces back up after dropping. It's called support because it's a level that keeps the price of a security from falling further, i.e., it's a price where most investors think that a security is a good buy.

Resistance level are price levels at which most investors tend to sell off their holdings. This may indicate that in general, investors feel that at these levels, securities are already expensive and their prices are primed for a fall or correction, hence the sell-off.

A good illustration of why these two levels are important is a floor and a ceiling or roof. Support levels are floors while resistance levels are ceilings or roofs.

When you're standing at the second floor of a building or a house, you will not be able to crash back down to the ground floor. The floor supports you so that you go no lower than the second floor, regardless of how hard you jump or stomp on it.

Unless the floor is made of weak materials, you weight will hold and you'll never go lower than the second floor. But if it's weak, you'll breach or break through the floor beneath you and you'll come crashing down to the first floor. In the same manner, when prices of securities breach or fall below established support levels, their upward trends end and a downward one begins.

Resistance levels, on the other hand, are like ceilings or roofs that keep a helium filled balloon from going higher. You can pull the balloon down and let it go but it will never go higher than the ceiling or roof.

But if the ceiling or roof is removed or if you bring the balloon outside where the roof or ceiling doesn't provide any cover, the balloon is free to fly. In the same manner, resistance levels keep prices from soaring and when prices break through them, their bearish trend may end and a bullish one may begin in its stead.

When it comes to price charts, the ability to properly identify strong support and resistance levels is key because they're the demarcation lines that will tell you whether or not a current trend is likely to continue so you can take profitable swing trading positions.

In case you may have already forgotten from the first book, support levels or support lines are drawn by connecting consecutive price valleys or troughs with a straight line. Resistance lines are drawn by connecting consecutive peaks or high prices with a straight line, too.

And when prices go below or above support or resistance lines, respectively, a trend reversal is highly likely to happen or may have already happened. If a security's price is on a downtrend and its price breaches above a strongly established resistance line, it may indicate that the downward trend has already ended and an upward one has already begun.

Support and resistance lines can also help you identify price bands or price ranges. These refer to the range in which a security's price typically vacillate. Price bands can be very useful when a security's price is in consolidation mode, i.e., moving sideways. The upper band, i.e., the resistance line, gives you an idea of when to sell and the lower band, i.e., the support line, gives you an idea of when to buy. You can profit from multiple trades of one security that's moving sideways in a relatively defined price range or band.

Chapter 3

Fundamental and Technical Analysis
- A Dynamic Duo

It used to be that fundamental and technical analysts would butt heads over which of the two financial securities analysis methods are superior. And probably to some extent, such butting of heads continue today. But instead of pitting one against another, the best investment and trading strategy is a marriage of the two, i.e., fundamental + technical analysis instead of fundamental vs. technical analysis.

Fundamental analysis answers the question of which securities are best for trading or investing based on their fundamental financial information and value. However, it doesn't tell you when is the optimal time to take or close positions in said securities.

On the other hand, technical analysis answers the question when to buy or sell securities. However, it doesn't tell you whether securities have a solid foundation for taking positions in. In short, it can tell you to buy junk securities of companies that are about to go under.

Fundamental analysis makes the buying or selling signals identified via technical analysis much more reliable. When you use both fundamental and technical analysis, you get the benefit of optimally timing your positions in the most fundamentally sound securities. It's a very win-win situation.

There are many fundamental analysis ratios that can help identify which securities, stocks in particular, are very solid and are currently trading at bargain prices. However, you only need a couple of them: the P/E (price-earnings) and the ROE/ROI ratios. The P/E ratio tells you how cheap or expensive the current trading price of a stock is while the ROE/ROI ratio tells you how profitable a specific stock is compared to others.

While there's really no hard and fast rule about P/E ratios, a good benchmark is 10 times and below. This means stocks with a P/E ratio of 10 times or lower are generally considered cheap.

For return on equity/return on investment, good benchmarks are the average annual returns on stocks of similar/competitor companies, the industry, and the stock market.

Aside from these ratios, another important piece of fundamental information you can use to choose your securities, e.g., stocks, is news. Significant developments in the company that are broadcast in the news or significant economic or political developments that can impact a company's operations can significantly influence a security's possible price swing.

In the following chapters, we'll discuss the different technical analysis strategies for timing your swing trades based on the stocks you've shortlisted via fundamental analysis.

Chapter 4

Swing Trading Price Chart Patterns

Price chart patterns refer to shapes and patterns that prices form, which provide insights when trends are about to reverse or are on track to continue. Most swing trading strategies are predicated upon price chart patterns and/or technical indicators.

There are two general types of price patterns: reversal patterns and continuation patterns. Considering that the most popular type of price chart used by traders is the Japanese candlestick chart, the price patterns we'll discuss will all be applicable to this type of chart.

Reversal Patterns

The Head and Shoulders Pattern

This pattern involves three consecutive price peaks, with the second peak being the highest (the head) and the first and third ones almost of the same height (the shoulders flanking the head). This pattern's applicable to a bullish or upward trending security and may signal the end or reversal of such trend.

When the price falls below the support line of this pattern, it's highly probable that the bullish trend has ended and that a bearish one has begun. How do you draw the support line? Connect the left and right bases or troughs of the "head" with a line and extending it.

The breach's accuracy can be optimized if accompanied by substantially higher than usual trading volume, which indicates a great number of investors have started to unload the stock already.

The Reverse Head and Shoulders Pattern

As the name implies, this is the inverse or upside down of the head and shoulders pattern. This pattern occurs in a bearish or downward trending security or market. This pattern consists of three consecutive valleys, lows, or troughs, with the second or middle valley being the lowest and the first and third valleys or troughs being of approximately the same depth.

The bearish pattern is considered to have ended when a security's price has breached an established resistance level, which is established by connecting the base of the neck of the "head" with a straight line and extending it.

As with the standard head and shoulders, substantially heavier trading volume than the usual helps establish the identified trend reversal even more. It means a great number of investors have already taken long positions on the security, which was the driving force that pushed the security's price above the established resistance and reverse the bearish trend.

The Double or Triple Top Pattern

These two patterns occur in bullish or upward trending securities or markets and are characterized by consecutive peaks of roughly the same height. For double tops, it is two consecutive and similarly-heighted peaks, while for triple tops, it's three consecutive ones.

The reversal is confirmed when the security's price falls below the established support line. This line is established by connecting the previous low and the valley between the twin peaks for double tops with a straight line and extending that line. For triple tops, the support line's established by connecting the two valleys between the three tops with a straight line and extending it.

The breach's accuracy can be optimized if accompanied by substantially higher than usual trading volume, which indicates a great number of investors have already started to unload the stock.

The Double or Triple Bottom Pattern

This is the exact opposite or inverse of the double and triple top patterns and occurs in bearish or downward trending securities or markets. It's characterized by two consecutive valleys, lows, or troughs of roughly the same depth for double bottoms and three consecutive ones for triple bottoms.

A reversal is deemed to have already occurred when the price of a security breaches above the established resistance line. For double bottoms, the resistance line's established by connecting the last peak before the first bottom and the peak between the two valleys or bottoms with a straight line and extending that line.

Substantially heavier trading volume than the usual helps establish the identified trend reversal even more. It means a great number of investors have already taken long positions on the security, which was the driving force that pushed the security's price above the established resistance and reverse the bearish trend.

Continuation Patterns

As the name implies, these patterns signal the resumption of an existing trend, which may have stalled for a while as prices started moving sideways, i.e., consolidating.

Triangles

Triangle patterns occur as part of a security price's consolidation phase during which, prices move up and down such that succeeding peaks become lower while succeeding lows become higher, resulting in a narrowing price band that resembles a triangle.

There are three kinds of triangle continuation patterns: symmetric, ascending and descending. Symmetric triangles are formed by a downward sloping resistance line and an upward sloping support line. An ascending triangle is one with a relatively flat resistance line and an upward sloping support line while a descending triangle is formed by a relatively flat support line and downward sloping resistance line.

For a triangle to form, a minimum of two peaks and lows each is needed. The nearer a triangle's apex is to the price, the higher the chance that it's about to break out. If the price eventually breaks out of the triangle towards the same direction as the existing trend, then it's a confirmation that the current trend has resumed, which can be a good opportunity to take positions in a security.

Flags

When a security's price moves within a band composed of almost parallel resistance and support lines, a flag pattern is formed. When prices break out of the bands in the direction of the existing trend, it indicates that the consolidation phase has ceased and the current trend has resumed.

Flags can be upward sloping (during bearish trends) or downward sloping (during bullish trends).

Rectangles

Similar to flags, rectangles are formed when prices move in a band where the support and resistance lines are parallel or nearly parallel.

The only difference is that rectangles have little or no slope, i.e., flat. As with flags, the current trend is considered to have resumed when prices break out of the rectangular band towards the direction of the existing trend, which is a good opportunity to take a position in the security.

Chapter 5

The Japanese Candlestick Price Chart

The Japanese candlestick chart is a kind of chart populated by prices that look like, well, Japanese candles. Each time period entry, e.g., daily, weekly, or hourly security price, constitutes one candlestick, which reflects four types of price information, mainly:

1. Previous period's opening price;

2. Previous period's closing price;

3. Previous period's highest price; and

4. Previous period's lowest price.

Each candlestick has a hollow body, the top and bottom of which represents the opening and closing prices for that time period. If the opening price is higher than the closing, then the top part of the hollow body represents the opening price and the bottom part the closing, and vice-versa.

If the security's closing price for that period was higher than its opening, the body is colored white, which indicates buying pressure. If it closed at a lower price than its opening, it's colored red, which indicates selling pressure.

Because candlesticks won't be such without wicks, a Japanese candlestick has wicks, too, which protrude above and/or below the hollow body. The top of the upper wick represents the highest price for that particular period while the bottom of the lower wick represents the lowest price for that period.

One reason why Japanese candlesticks are very popular among traders is because they can immediately see what happened to a security's price in just one look. If colored white, it means that buying pressure was stronger than selling pressure during that time period while a red colored candle means greater selling pressure than buying. Also, the length of the wick from the top of the upper wick to the bottom of the lower one shows how volatile the price of a security was during that time period. A long Japanese candlestick means a great difference between the highest and lowest price for that period, i.e., high volatility. A short candlestick means a small difference between the high and low prices, i.e., low volatility.

Japanese Candlestick Swing Trading Patterns

The following are some of the most popular candlestick patterns for taking or closing positions.

The Three-Line Strike Pattern

This pattern occurs within a downtrend, which signals its reversal to a bullish one. This is characterized by three consecutively lower red (or in other charts, black) candlesticks. Each candlestick registers successively lower "low" prices and closes close its intrabar low price. The fourth candlestick opens at an even lower price than the third red candle but eventually closes higher than the high price of the first red candlestick of the series. Also, the opening price for the fourth bar is also its lowest for that period. In 84% of the time, this patterns results in reversals according to the author of the premier candlestick analysis book Encyclopedia of Candlestick Charts, Thomas Bulkowski.

Because it signals a reversal of a bearish pattern, you can use this as a swing trading signal for either taking a long position or closing a short one.

The Abandoned Baby

This pattern usually occurs near or at the end of a downtrend, which is characterized by a series of red/black candles with consecutively lower lows followed by Doji candlestick that gaps downward, then by an upward-gapping candlestick. A Doji candlestick is one whose opening and closing prices are the same, hence making the body flat and the stick resemble a cross.

Per Bulkowski, the abandoned baby pattern has a 70% accuracy rate, making it a good trading signal for either taking a long position or closing a short one.

The Two-Red (or Black) Gapping Pattern

This bull reversal pattern appears right after a significant peak price of a security. This is characterized by two red or black candles that have a downward gap in between, with each red or black candle registering lower lows. This pattern predicts that the price drop will continue and become even more pronounced, which may ultimately trigger a longer downtrend in a security's price. According to Thomas Bulkowski, the two-red/black gapping pattern has an accuracy rate of about 68%, making it a fairly reliable swing trading signal to either take a short position or close a long one.

The Three Red Crows Pattern

This pattern occurs near the top of an uptrend and is characterized by three consecutive red candlesticks with successively lower lows and closing prices that are close to their intra-candlestick lows. This pattern forecasts an extended decline in a security's price to even lower lows, which may eventually trigger a long-term bearish trend.

This pattern has an accuracy rate of about 78% per Bulkowski, which makes it a good swing trading signal to either take a short position or close a long one.

Chapter 6

Technical Indicators

The challenge with price chart patterns is that they can be subjective, i.e., the patterns may be in the eyes of the beholder. While patterns are fairly reliable, it can happen that some traders see a specific pattern while others don't, particularly for patterns that aren't so obvious. This is where technical indicators come in.

Technical indicators are statistical metrics or figures that are computed based on a security's past price movements. Because they're based on numbers, they're not as subjective as price chart reading. And as such, technical indicators can provide a more objective basis for position entry and exit points.

There's a myriad number of technical indicators that multitudes of traders use and you might just lose interest, not to mention your mind, if you try to study each of them before choosing. Fortunately, you don't need to use a lot of indicators to swing trade successfully. You'll only need a couple of them.

Many newbie swing traders wonder if it's more beneficial to use both price charts and technical indicators or just one of the two. In most cases, it's really just a matter of personal preference. Those who are more numbers-driven may prefer to stick to technical indicators while some who are more intuitive may choose to stick to price charts. I believe using both is a good way to start trading and as you go along, you'll get a better feel of what works better for you, i.e., using both or one or the other.

The following are some of the most popular technical indicators used by traders all over the world, be it for day trading or swing trading.

Simple Moving Average

When you look at price charts, you don't see a smooth price movement pattern but a relatively jagged one. This can make identifying patterns very challenging, especially during very volatile market conditions.

Moving averages can help you look at those prices in smoother and more discernable pattern as it smooths out the rough edges by mathematically averaging prices for the last number of time periods. The reason it's called "moving" is because every succeeding period, a new average price is computed based on the previous X number of time periods.

For example, a 90-day moving average means that it's the average for the last 90 trading days. Tomorrow, the last 90 trading days will be different than today's, hence the term "moving". The most common price used for moving averages is the day's closing price. But traders like you can use the last trading price every 5, 15, or 30 minutes, which is what day traders use. But given the time horizon of swing trading, daily closing prices are the most appropriate.

How can you use moving averages to time your swing trades? Look for crossovers, which is when a moving average goes above or below a security's actual price or another moving average period.

If you only use one moving average period, there are two ways crossovers happen. The first is during bearish or downward trends. When a security is in a bearish trend, the moving average will be higher than the actual price. When the moving actual price crosses over and above the moving average for that period, it can be taken as a sign that the bearish trend has officially ended, i.e., a buy signal.

On the other hand, the actual price is higher than the moving average figure during bullish or upward trends. When a security's actual price crosses the moving average and goes below it, this signals that the bullish trend has really reversed and the current trend is now a bearish one, i.e., a sell signal.

Now, you can also use two moving averages to confirm trend reversals. In which case, the shorter period moving average will be higher than the longer period moving average during a bullish trend and it will be lower than the longer period moving average during a bearish trend.

When the shorter period moving average crosses below the longer period moving average, it means that the bullish trend has already ended and that a bearish one has already begun (sell signal). When the shorter period moving average crosses above the longer period moving average during a bearish trend, it's a signal that the trend has ended and that a bullish one has already begun (buy signal).

How many days should you use for your moving averages? It depends on your risk appetite. The shorter the moving average time period, the more sensitive it is to price movements and therefore, it can help you identify possible trend reversals faster.

However, there's a catch to such high sensitivity. It's also more prone to false reversal signals, i.e., whiplashes, which can cause you to take ill-timed positions in securities.

On the other hand, a longer period moving average is less sensitive to actual price volatility and therefore, is less prone to whiplashes. However, it will take more time to identify a trend reversal, which can also put you at risk of ill-timed positions, albeit the risk is much lower compared with much shorter period moving averages.

How do you figure out which period to use for moving averages? Well, it depends on your security. Check out its historical prices and generate moving averages for several time periods, e.g., 10, 15, 20, 30, 50, 60, and 90 day moving averages. Check out which of them has the very few or no whiplashes. In the event that there are more than or 2 moving average periods that provide minimal or no whiplashes, choose the shortest one or two (depending on how many you plan to use) because shorter period moving averages allow you to identify trend reversals faster.

Exponential Moving Averages

A simple moving average assigns equal weight to all price data used in computing for the average price for X number of days. This means that the oldest price data is viewed as having the same relevance or significance as the most recent price data.

With an exponential moving average, each of the price data points have different weights or relevance in computing for the moving average. To be more specific, the most recent price data holds the greatest relevance or weight while the oldest price data holds the least. From the most recent to the oldest, each data point's weight or relevance gradually becomes less.

The same principle as the simple moving average applies to the exponential moving average: i.e., during bull runs, shorter moving averages run above a longer-period moving average and below the actual security price. During bear markets, shorter-period moving averages run below longer-period ones and above the security's actual price.

A bull market is considered to have ended (sell signal) when the shorter-period moving average crosses below the longer-period one and when it crosses above the security's actual price. A bear market is considered to have ended (buy signal) when the shorter-period moving average crosses above the longer-period one and below the security's actual price.

Bollinger Bands

Finding points on which trends reverse is crucial for swing trading success. But equally important is finding reliable support and resistance lines. For the latter, Bollinger bands can be a very great help.

Bollinger bands are dynamic, i.e., they change every day according to actual movements in the security's price. Therefore, the price bands, i.e., support and resistance levels, reflect the most recent price movements and their momentum and change daily. This may be considered as a more accurate and objective way of determining support and resistance levels compared to drawing static lines on price charts.

There are three parts to a Bollinger band: The upper band, the lower band, and the middle. The middle part is the simple moving average line, the default period of which is usually set to 20 days but you can set it differently according to your trading platform. The upper band, i.e., the resistance level, is two standard deviations above the moving average. The lower band, i.e., the support level, is two standard deviations below the moving average.

What's the significance of the upper and lower bands? When a security's actual price is very close to one of the bands, it means that the security is already overbought (if close to the upper band) or oversold (if close to the lower band). If a security is already oversold, selling pressure has already weakened to the point that buying pressure can start pushing prices up. If a security is already overbought, it means that buying pressure has already weakened to the point that selling pressure has become greater and is already pushing prices down.

What about overbought and oversold? When a security is already oversold and prices go below the lower part of the Bollinger band, it's a good time to enter and take a long position or close a short position because the bulls are already in control. When a security is already overbought and a security's price goes above the upper Bollinger band, it's a good time to either take short position or close an open long position.

However, it's not wise to rely solely on the Bollinger bands to time your swing trades. The best way to use it is in accordance with other indicators and price chart patterns. The Bollinger band should merely be an additional metric for consideration.

The width of the Bollinger band indicates how volatile a security's price is. The wider the band, the higher the volatility and vice-versa.

True and Average True Ranges

True range is computed according to your preferred time period, e.g., daily, hourly, weekly, etc. It's based on the highest amount between three quantities, namely:

1. The difference between the current period's highest and lowest prices;

2. The difference between the previous period's closing price and the current one's highest price; and

3. The difference in the previous period's closing price and the current period's lowest price.

True range is more of a measure of volatility of a security's price. The true ranges for consecutive trading periods can then be averaged ala-

simple moving average. This moving average is the average true range, which increases as a security's price becomes more volatile and decreases when it becomes less volatile.

Average true range is useful for determining exit points only, not entry ones. Also, it doesn't give ideas about a security's price direction. It only focuses on volatility.

The average true range is used by the Chandelier Exit of determining ideal position exit points. This is done by calculating a specific multiple for the true range then deducting it from the highest peak price that occurred after taking a position in a security. The Chandelier exit typically functions as a means to determine a stop-loss point, which normally uses a multiple of three times the average true range deducted from the highest post entry peak price.

Directional Moving Index (DMI) and Average Directional Index (ADX)

When you swing trade according to the direction of a strong trend, you can minimize your risk for losses and maximize your chances for trading profits. You can use the ADX technical indicator to get a good estimate of the strength of a security price's current trend. Many traders consider the ADX to be the ultimate price trend technical indicator.

The ADX helps quantify or put into numbers the strength of a security's price trend. Computed ADX figures use the directional movement index (DMI) of a security's price over a specific time frame. Usually, traders use 14 bars (time periods, e.g., days) but you can use any time period you want.

You can plot the computer or platform generated ADX figures as a single line, the values of which can be as low as zero and as high as 100. The average directional index, ironically, is a non-directional technical indicator because it measures the strength of an existing trend, not its direction. In most cases, traders plot the ADX in the same as the DMI (directional movement indicator lines) from which it's computed from.

The DMI, on the other hand, is a technical indicator that tells you the direction of the current trend of a security's price. The DMI tells you this by comparing previous high and low prices and drawing two lines. These lines are the positive directional movement line (+DI) and the negative directional movement line (-DI).

When the +DI is above the -DI, this means that the buying or upward pressure on a security's price is greater than the downward or selling pressure. Hence, it means that the security's price is trending upward.

On the other hand, downward or selling pressure's greater than the upward or buying pressure when the +DI is below the -DI. Hence, it means that a security's price is trending downward.

Swing traders often use DMI crossovers as trading signals. When the +DMI crosses below the -DMI line, it signals that the upward trend has ended and a downward one has begun, which means one must sell the security. When the +DMI line crosses above the -DMI line, it means the downtrend has ended and an uptrend has already begun, which means one can start taking long positions (buy) that security.

The ADX may be considered as the third line, and it shows the difference between the two DI lines. This difference indicates the strength of a current trend. Hence, it's always in the middle of the +DI and -DI lines. As mentioned earlier, its value ranges between zero to 100, with zero being the weakest and 100 being the strongest measure of a trend's strength.

So, an ADX of 90 when the +DI is below the -DI line means that current selling pressure or the current downward trend is very strong.

Hence, you can reasonably expect the price of that security to drop even further, at least in the near term.

An ADX of 90 when the +DI line's above the -DI one means that the current upward trend of a security is very strong. As such, you may reasonably expect that security's price to continue its upward direction, at least in the near term.

The ADX helps you prepare for a highly-probable trend reversal so you can either act as soon as a crossover happens or pre-empt the market by taking a pre-emptive position already just before a trend reverses. When the ADX shows a current trend weakening, it indicates a high possibility of a near-term trend reversal and a good swing trading opportunity for your short-listed securities.

Within the spectrum of zero to 100, how do you quantify the strength of a current trend? The following are the range of ADX values and the corresponding trend strength levels:

1. Zero to 25 means no trend or weak trend;

2. Above 25 to 50 means a strong trend;

3. Above 50 to 75 means a very strong trend; and

4. Above 75 to 100 means an extremely strong trend.

A low ADX number normally means that investors are already accumulating (during a downtrend) or distributing (during an uptrend) a security, which means a trend reversal may be in the works soon. A below-25 ADX figure for more than 30 trading periods, e.g., days, a security's price patterns often become easier to identify, moves between a specific price range to find buyer and seller interest, and eventually break out into a trend.

While the ADX line doesn't show the direction of a current trend, it does show the direction of the strength of the trend, i.e., if it's getting weaker or stronger. When the ADX line is sloping upward, the current trend is getting stronger and vice versa.

One thing you'll need to remember about the ADX is that a weakening trend doesn't necessarily mean a trend reversal's about to happen soon. Yes, there's a good chance that it's coming but in many cases, it may simply means that the current trend is just weakening or taking a break before resuming its direction. A good way to know whether downward trending ADX is a signal of an impending trend reversal is if it's accompanied by a price climax, which is usually characterized by a substantial increase in trading volume and substantial price jumps or drops.

When you know a security's price trend is increasing, you can enter a position, add to your current position, or maintain your current position so you can maximize your potential swing trading profits as the trend continues. However, when you see successively lower ADX highs or peaks, consider them as a reminder to start watching a security's prices and exercise more control over your risks.

You can also use the ADX to identify momentum divergences, i.e., when the price of a security and its ADX go on different directions. For example, when a security's high price continues to increase but the ADX highs continues to decrease, it's called a negative divergence, a.k.a., non-confirmation. This doesn't necessarily mean an impending trend reversal but a signal that the strength or momentum of the current price trend is changing. You can take this as a cue to start taking partial profits on your existing positions or lower your stop-loss limits.

The best swing trading strategy using the ADX is to use it as a confirmation or auxiliary decision-making basis rather than the primary. In particular, analyze a security's price chart or movements first before analyzing or reading its ADX within the context of the price chart. Essentially, technical indicators should supplement you with information that security prices may not clearly show or give.

A good example of this are price breakouts. These normally happen after a price consolidation phase, i.e., buying and selling pressure are almost equal and prices move sideways in a relatively defined band. When one side overpowers the other, the balance of power between supply and demand tips over and a price breakout happens.

However, price breakouts can be very challenging to spot or validate based on price charts alone. This is where a technical indicator like the ADX can come in and provide supplemental information that can validate or invalidate what may appear to be a price breakout based on price chart movements. How?

Let's say the stock price of Company A, which has been consolidating between $1.00 and $1.50 per share in the last two weeks breaks out upward to $1.65. If the ADX crosses over from below 25 (weak or no trend) to above 25 (strong trend), it means that the upward price breakout is supported by strong momentum. This means that the upward breakout will most likely continue as an uptrend, which is a good time to take a long swing trading position.

You can also use the ADX as a swing trading range finder. Based on price charts alone, it can also be very challenging to identify when a security's price trend has paused and has already entered a consolidation phase or range. When a security's ADX drops from above 25 (strong) to below 25 (weak or no trend), it means that in general, buyers and sellers have agreed to a specific price range for a security. This should be a signal to be more vigilant and watchful for an impending price breakout so you can time your new positions or manage your existing ones optimally.

Chapter 7

Swing Trading Psychology

S wing trading strategies, like the ones we've discussed, are very important for swing trading success. However, they're just account for half of your potential success. The other half is your swing trading psychology. Without it, even the best trading strategies in the world may not work for you. In this chapter, we'll take a look at some of the most important swing trading psychological practices you'll need to get down to pat to optimize your trading strategies' ability to give you meaningful profits.

Learn to Be Comfortable with Small Losses

As a swing trader, one of the toughest things you'll need to learn to live with are trading losses. No trader, even the best ones in the world, are immune to trading losses. It's a part of life.

However, many traders' emotions can get out of control when they lose trades, especially relatively big ones and when they activate their stop-loss limits then the security changes directions and eventually hits their price targets, making them regret their stop-loss actions. When this happens, many traders tend to let their emotions control their subsequent trades by trading with their emotions, micro-managing their trades, and losing objectivity.

You can minimize your risks for these by learning to take small hits or losses instead of bigger ones. This means a lower stop-loss limit, which is a good swing trading risk management practice. There are good reasons for this.

One is that small losses hurt much less. If they hurt much less, your risks for letting your emotions run your subsequent trades become lower.

Another good reason for learning to accept small losses is that you get to limit the size of your trading losses, particularly if your risk appetite's not that big. This means you get to preserve your trading capital much longer until you start getting the hang of swing trading and begin generating more swing trading profits than losses.

By learning to be comfortable with small losses, you get your skin in the game much longer.

Have a Long Term Perspective on Your Swing Trades

You can look at your swing trading efforts from a long-term perspective in two ways. First, you can set your expectations that it'll take you six months to a year to get the hang of it and start earning more trading profits than trading losses. That way, you won't begin and continue your initial swing trading efforts under pressure, which can make you make really bad swing trading decisions out of desperation.

Another way you can swing trade with a long-term perspective is to think in terms of your first 10, 20, 50, or even 100 swing trades! If you start day trading by focusing on the results of each and every trade, you just might make you go swing trading crazy and lead making foolish and impulsive swing trading decisions.

If you focus on every trade and evaluate your success based one trade at a time, even a small loss, which is expected, can lead you to conclude that your swing trading strategy's a fluke and make you jump from one strategy to another without really giving each strategy enough time and trades to master and validate. By jumping from one strategy to another after every loss or two, you'll never be able to master any swing trading strategy, ever.

Just like how your professors graded you in school based on the average of your multiple quizzes, exams, and recitations, you should also evaluate your swing trading success or shortcomings within the context of many swing trades.

Swing Trade According to Your Risk Appetite

There's no denying the fact that you can risk losing money by swing trading. Remember, the higher the expected return on your investments, the higher your financial risks. Because swing trading can give you potentially superior returns compared to bank deposits and other fixed income securities, the financial risks are also higher.

Many traders trade emotionally out of fear. Most of the time, the fear comes from the fact that they're not comfortable losing a certain amount of money. Maybe it's because their swing trading capital is an amount of money they'll need in the foreseeable future, which means they can't afford to lose some or all of it. Or maybe they're just not comfortable with losing a certain sum of money.

If you're like that, your best bet would be to limit your swing trading capital to an amount of money that you're comfortable losing, especially when you're just starting out. That way, you can minimize your risks for emotional trading, e.g., fear-driven trading, and optimize your chances of swing trading profitably.

Another important reason for trading based on your risk appetite is fiscal security. If you trade more than what you can afford to lose, you risk sacrificing your ability to meet some or most of your personal or family needs. The amount of money you should dedicate for swing trading must be that which, if lost entirely, will not have a significant impact on your personal or family finances. Never allocate your emergency fund or your kid's tuition fee money next year for swing trading today. Swing trade only your excess money.

Don't Be Greedy

Either way, emotional trading is foolish. On one end of the spectrum is fear-based trading. On the other end is being greedy.

When you're greedy, you'll always go for one-time-big-time profits and will not settle for small ones. The problem with this approach is that one-time-trading profits are very hard to accomplish and opportunities for such rarely come by. Greed can make you lose more trades than you win because even winning trades can eventually become losses when greed keeps you from exiting while ahead because prices eventually drop as you continue waiting for unreasonably higher profits.

This has happened to me before. I took a long position on stocks of a prominent real-estate company and after 2 weeks, I was up 30%. But I truly believed, or wanted to believe, that it could still go up and give me at least 50% return in less than a month.

On the third week, the price dropped such that I was still up but only by 20%. "No matter, it's just a correction and it'll resume its upward trend in a few days." I thought to myself. On the fourth week, I was only up by 10% and by the end of the fifth week, I was down 5%. All that time, I kept convincing myself "It's just a correction." I eventually had to liquidate at a loss of 15%. From gold to garbage – and it's all because of my greed.

Set modest swing trading gains and once your security's price hits your target, liquidate your position. At the very least, liquidate a good portion of it, say 50%. That way, you end up breaking even at worst if the price subsequently drops.

Take Smaller Positions

Another way by which you can keep swing trading greed in check is by taking smaller swing trading positions. How does it help you do that?

Setting unrealistic swing trading targets is just one way greed rears its ugly head. The other way it does is through large position sizes. This is because even if you set modest profit price targets, you can magnify your potential trading profits by going for large trading positions. For example, you can earn a trading profit of $1,000 through:

1. Profit per share of only $0.50 with a position size of 2,000 shares; or

2. Profit per share of $1.00 with a position size of 1,000 shares only.

You can double your potential trading profit by doubling your position size! However, you also risk twice the loss by doing so.

Just because you've allotted a swing trading amount within your risk appetite doesn't mean you should put it all in one security in hopes of raking in a windfall. Aside from setting modest profit price targets, keep your position sizes modest, too, by diversifying your swing trading capital across several securities in smaller position sizes.

Conclusion

I hope that you've learned a lot about principles and strategies for swing trading successfully. But more than just learning, I hope you're excited to them out soon. You see, knowing's just half the battle for successful swing trading. The other half's action or application of knowledge. That's why I want to encourage you to start applying what you learned here as soon as possible, so you'll minimize your risks for inaction.

You don't have to apply everything at once. Focus on one or two learnings first. Once you've gotten a good handle on those, apply the others one or two at a time. Remember, Rome wasn't built in a day but the Romans were busy laying bricks by the hour. It took time to build the empire. So will it be with your swing trading empire – it'll take time and consistent practice.

Here's to your swing trading success my friend! Cheers!

References

A) https://www.investopedia.com/articles/active-trading/092315/5-most-powerful-candlestick-patterns.asp

B) https://bullsonwallstreet.com/5-tips-improve-trading-psychology/

C) https://www.investopedia.com/articles/trading/07/adx-trend-indicator.asp

SWING TRADING

Advanced and Effective Strategies to Execute Swing Trading

WILLIAM RILEY

Introduction

Swing trading is one of the most exciting ways to make serious money. It's because, aside from the enormous potential for making good money without having to slave away, it's also something you can do from the comfort of your own home. You can also do it from a coffee shop, on the bus, at the beach, or anywhere that has good access to the Internet. Now, what can be more exciting than that, eh?

In this book, the assumption is you're already familiar with swing trading and technical analysis in general. Hence, it'll focus on six strategies that can help you maximize your chances of swing trading profitably and making good money. On top of these six strategies, I'll also share how to maximize your chances of profitably executing swing trades and some important general tips that will help you with this.

So, if you're ready, turn the page and let's begin!

Chapter 1

The Fibonacci Retracement Strategy

The Fibonacci sequence is a set of sequential numbers that begin with a zero or a one. These numbers are followed by a one, then by the sum of the two preceding numbers.

An example of a Fibonacci sequence of numbers would be:

- 0;
- 1 (the sum of 0 since there is only one preceding number for this number, which is zero);
- 1 (the sum of the two preceding numbers, 0 and 1);
- 2 (the sum of the two preceding numbers, 1 and 1);
- 3 (the sum of the two preceding numbers, 2 and 1);
- 5 (the sum of the two preceding numbers, 2 and 3); and
- 8 (the sum of the two preceding numbers, 3 and 5).

This numeric sequence was conceptualized by an Italian guy named, surprise, Fibonacci a.k.a. Leonardo Pisano. Fibonacci was born in 1170 and grew up in Bugia, he studied mathematics, and he learned much about the Hindu-Arabic number system, including its advantages.

In 1202, Fibonacci documented his learnings right after he returned to his native Italy. The document has been famously known as Liber Abaci, roughly translated as the Book of Abacus. This book made using Hindu-Arabic numbers in the European continent easy. Fibonacci first described the now-famous number sequence named after him in his Liber Abaci.

As mentioned earlier, the Fibonacci sequence involved a series of numbers that started with either 0 or 1, where each succeeding number was the sum of its two immediately-preceding numbers. In our example earlier, it was 0, 1, 1, 2, 3, 5, and 8. The Fibonacci sequence can be extended to infinity, and each of the numbers in the sequence is about 1.618 times bigger than the number before. This number is often referred to as the Golden Ratio or Phi, and its inverse is 0.618.

What's the big deal about the Golden Ratio? Well, it appears that the ratio naturally occurs in the natural world, biology, fine arts, and even architecture. Some of the places where one can find the Golden Ratio at work include:

- Ancient Greek vases;
- Branches of trees;
- Human faces;
- Rose petals;
- Shells of mollusks;
- Spiral galaxies of the universe;
- Sunflowers;
- The Mona Lisa; and
- The Parthenon.

Fibonacci in Financial Markets

The Fibonacci principle is also present and used in financial market trading activities. However, trading doesn't directly involve numbers that make up the Fibonacci sequence. Instead, the Fibonacci principle applies to financial markets in terms of the numerical relationship between a sequence's numbers. In particular, financial market trading makes use of the Golden Ratio's inverse, i.e., 0.618 or 61.8%.

The Fibonacci ratio for between a number and another number two sequences after it (to the right) is approximately 38.2%. And if you divide a number in the sequence by the third number after it (to the right), you'll get a Fibonacci ratio of 23.6%.

Now, what's the point of these Fibonacci ratios when it comes to swing trading? It's used in a swing trading strategy called Fibonacci retracement. This strategy involves estimating price retracement points based on established high and low prices. From these high and low prices, traders estimate retracement levels using the three ratios earlier: 23.6%, 38.2%, and 61.8%. These ratios help traders produce horizontal price grids that act as support and/or resistance lines, i.e., price reversal points.

A 50% price retracement level, while not a Fibonacci ratio, is often used by traders simply because it's a psychologically important price reversal point. This was pointed out in both the work of technical analysis pioneer, W.D. Gann, as well as in the infamous Dow Theory.

Fibonacci retracement price levels are frequently incorporated in trend-trading strategies. When traders perceive a possible retracement is occurring within an identified trend, they usually attempt to take low-risk positions consistent with the general direction of the initial trend they're following based on estimated Fibonacci retracement levels. Traders who do this believe that the chances are high that when a financial security's (e.g., stock) price hits a retracement level during a correction phase, it'll bounce back and resume its original trend.

Let's take a look at an example so you can get a clearer idea of how to use the Fibonacci retracement strategy for your swing trades. Stock A's on an uptrend, and its most recent peak and low prices are $20 and $10 per share, respectively. As of last week, the share price of Stock A had been going down from its last peak of $20 per share.

The Fibonacci retracement levels for Stock A as of the moment are as follows:

- A 23.6% retracement from $20 is $15.28, i.e., $20 – ($20 X 23.6%);

- A 38.2% retracement from $20 is $12.36, i.e., $20 – ($20 X 38.2%); and

- A 61.8% retracement from $20 is $7.64, i.e., $20 – ($20 X 61.8%).

So, when the price of Stock A touches $15.28, you buy its shares because based on the Fibonacci retracement principle, the chances are high that it will bounce back up from this level. But since it's not a perfect strategy, there's a likelihood still that the price might drop down further, hence the two other retracement levels of $12.36 and $7.64.

That's why another good swing trading strategy that's often paired up with the Fibonacci retracement is cost-averaging. Under the cost averaging strategy, you won't put all your chips in a stock at just one price point. Cost averaging means buying more shares or units of financial security at successively lower prices. By doing this, you can minimize your risk of losing trades and increase your potential swing trading profits even if share prices drop further after your first or second position-taking.

Here's how cost-averaging looks. Using Stock A again as our example, let's say you have $10,000 to invest in Stock A, and once its price hits the first retracement level of $15.28, you buy as many shares as you can with $10,000. At this price, you'll be able to buy 654 shares. If the retracement level holds at this point and the Stock A's price bounces right back, you'll be making money in no time at all.

But what if the price of Stock A dropped further to the second retracement level of $12.36? You can't buy any more shares, and you'll have to wait longer before its price gets back to the first retracement level of $15.28[1] Just to break even. To make a profit, you'll have to wait until Stock A's price exceeds $15.28 per share.

If you employ cost-averaging with Fibonacci retracement, you can divide your trading money among two or all of the three retracement levels. For simplicity's sake, let's say you divided your $10,000 trading money for Stock A into $3,333.33 for each retracement level.

When Stock A's price hit the first retracement level of $15.28, you buy up to 218 shares for $3,331. Your average cost per share of Stock A at this point is $15.28, which is your break-even mark. If it bounces back and resumes its upward trend, you make money immediately.

But if its price falls further to the second retracement level of $12.36 per share, you can buy $3,333.33 worth of Stock A again. The maximum number of shares you can buy at this price is 269 shares worth $3,325.

Now, you have a total of 487 shares of Stock A at a total cost of $6,656 for an average cost of $13.67 per share, which is your new breakeven point. You no longer have to wait for Stock A's share price to go back to $15.28 per share just to breakeven because your average cost went down to only $13.67. When Stock A's price goes back up to $15.28, you'd already have a nice trading profit. If the price hits the third retracement level and you buy more shares at that price, you'll bring down your average cost per share even further.

---

[1] Transactions costs, such as brokers' commissions, among others, are excluded in this example and others that'll follow for simplification purposes.

When using the Fibonacci retracement strategy, always keep in mind that the chances of price reversals of bounces from retracement levels are maximized when other technical indicators also signal a highly possible trend reversal. Some of the most popular reversal indicators you can use to confirm the strength of a retracement level are trend lines, candlestick patterns, moving averages, momentum oscillators, and trading volume. More supporting technical indicators there are, the more accurate a retracement level reversal is.

Fibonacci retracements can be used on many different trading time frames, e.g., daily, weekly, monthly, etc. It's important to remember that as with all other technical analysis indicators, the accuracy of Fibonacci retracement levels are proportionate to the duration or length of the time frames in which they're used. In particular, they're more accurate or valuable when used with longer time frames, e.g., a weekly Fibonacci retracement level of 23.6% is more accurate or probable than a daily Fibonacci retracement of the same ratio.

Extended Fibonacci Retracements

As they are, Fibonacci retracement levels are useful in terms of predicting potential support or resistance levels, i.e., price reversal points. These are used to determine possible position-taking and closing points for financial security, such as a stock.

Traders, like you, can use Fibonacci extensions to identify specific profit-taking price targets. But what are Fibonacci extensions?

These refer to levels that are drawn outside of the usual 100% price level. Traders like you can use Fibonacci extensions to set high potential profit-taking points in the direction of a current trend. If the major retracement levels are 23.6%, 38.2% and 61.8%, the major Fibonacci extensions are 161.8%, 261.8% and 423.6%.

How do you use these? Multiply the difference between the first two price points by a Fibonacci extension number. Then, add the resulting number to the third price point if the price projection is going upward or subtract from the third price point if the projection's downward.

For example, Stock A's previous high was $20 (1st price point), hit the first retracement level of $15.28 (2nd price point) before going back up to $17.50 per share (3rd price point). You can set a profit-taking target price by:

- Getting the difference between the first two price points, i.e., $20 - $15.28 = $4.72;

- Then, multiply the difference by a Fibonacci extension, e.g., $4.72 X 161.8% = $7.64; and

- Add the product to the third price point, e.g., $17.50 + 7.64 = $25.14.

Based on this example, you can set a profit-taking price target of $25.14 per share of Stock A.

Final Point on Fibonacci Retracement

While you can mark price reversal points with stunning accuracy using Fibonacci retracement levels, they can be quite challenging to execute, being an advanced swing trading strategy. The best way to use Fibonacci retracement levels is in conjunction with one or two more technical indicators to spot potentially low-risk but high-return potential swing trading opportunities.

Chapter 2

The Support and Resistance Trading Strategy

If you remember your basic technical analysis lessons, support and resistance levels are price levels that determine possible trend reversals. Support levels are those from which price levels tend to bounce back up from, i.e., it keeps a financial security's price from dropping further and allows an uptrend to continue. Resistance levels, on the other hand, are those from which prices bounce back down and keep a downtrend going. Support levels are like floors that keep something from falling down further, while resistance levels are ceilings that prevent something from flying away or going higher.

Traders use support and resistance levels as position-taking and closing points for trading, as well as to identify their personal risk levels. In general, traders use support and resistance levels like this:

1. Identify a specific price level or zone that has been historically established as a support or resistance level;

2. Assume that the market will start moving in the opposite direction;

3. Take positions accordingly, i.e., long position if reversal of a bearish trend at a support level or short position if reversal of a bullish trend at a resistance level; and

4. Set stop-loss limits below or above their position taking points.

While this makes perfect trading sense, it's probably not the best way to swing trade using support and resistance lines. Why?

Financial markets, such as the stock market, are dynamic. This makes levels-based trading akin to trading securities with your eyes closed. It can be very easy to discover specific price points that have established their validity as support or resistance levels in the past. In turn, this makes it very tempting to take trading positions or close them as soon as prices reach such levels.

This can be a very dangerous swing trading strategy. Why? Ask yourself the following questions before trading simply on seemingly established historical support and resistance levels:

1. When prices touch the same levels again, will the same traders be involved again?

2. Are market conditions exactly the same as the last time such price levels were reached?

3. Is the market context pretty much the same now as when such prices were reached in the past?

So, what's the point of talking about a support and resistance trading strategy? The kind of support or resistance levels involved in this strategy refers to neither mathematically generated levels nor trend lines. The kind of support and resistance levels involved in this swing trading strategy are those where trades have previously entered financial markets such that prices either started large swings or kept prices from falling or rising. These levels can:

1. Be strong just as they can be weak; and

2. Can fail just as much as they can hold.

At these levels, markets can turn back from them, breakthrough past them, or breakthrough then shortly afterward, reverses to resume the current trend (whiplashes or false breakouts). By studying trading actions around a specific price level, you can have a clear idea of the market context from which you can maximize your chances of finding great swing trading opportunities.

I mentioned earlier that the kinds of support and resistance levels we're talking about here aren't necessarily drawn trend lines. Why? For one, many long-time technical analysts and traders have already ditched using trend lines for establishing support and resistance levels. It's because there are certain challenges that come with using trend lines.

If you're a chartist who's been drawing trend lines for establishing support and resistance levels for a long time, you may be skeptical of what I'm saying here. You may even be offended. But herein lies the problem with using trend lines for this strategy: they're dynamic and subjective.

By dynamic, I mean drawing traditional trend lines by connecting previous peaks and troughs changes as time goes by. When a financial security's price establishes a new high or low, the corresponding slope of an upward or downward trend line will change in response to the new development. Basing your trading entry and exit points based on moving support and resistance lines is like building a 50-story building on shifting sand. It's risky and irresponsible.

By subjective, I mean trend lines differ from one technical analyst to another. It's kind of the same with deducing continuation and reversal patterns using trend lines. There were times when I saw a certain pattern – based on "established" trend lines (at least, in my mind) – that another trader didn't. There were times, too, that I couldn't see patterns that another trader saw.

Keep in mind that swing trading, which primarily relies on technical analysis for the timing of trades, is all about reading the market correctly. In short, it's about market psychology, and if you think differently than the market by assuming a certain trend line based on seemingly obvious peaks and troughs in the recent past, your swing trading dreams may eventually turn into a nightmare.

That being said, I'm not saying support and resistance lines are practically useless. What I'm driving at here is you'll need to draw them using much better ways - significantly less random and subjective ways. You can determine whether you're drawing a random trend line or not by:

1. Turning off your trading platform's charts' bars or candlesticks;

2. Draw horizontal lines on the chart at random; then

3. Turn on your charts or candlesticks again.

Now, look at your chart. Can you observe a specific price level/line from which the security's price seems to bounce back frequently? Do you notice a particular price where resistance and support levels seem to have swapped roles?

Once you find such horizontal "random" lines, how can you determine if they're more random than valid or vice-versa? A very good way to do this is by using what's called the "basic market trend structure." What does this structure look like?

1. Higher highs and lows indicate an upward or bullish trending security or market;

2. Lower highs and lows indicate a downward or bearish trending security or market; and

3. A market or security that's in range or consolidation will create both price actions.

Given the basic market trend structure, you can then define significant support or resistance levels by using the following guidelines:

1. Determine the trend, i.e., bearish, bullish, or range.

2. If the security's price is on a bullish trend, you can determine a POSSIBLE support level when:

   - Its price establishes a higher-high (HH);

   - Subsequent price movements bounce back down from this HH, i.e., acts as a resistance level; then

   - Shortly after, price action busts through this resistance level, turning it into a POSSIBLE support level.

3. If the security's price is on a bearish trend, you can determine a POSSIBLE resistance level when:

   - Its price establishes a lower-low (LL);

   - Subsequent price movements bounce back up from this LL, i.e., acts as a support level; then

   - Shortly after, price action busts down through this support level, turning it into a POSSIBLE resistance level.

You must take into consideration the amount of trading volume that happens when prices hit or bust through estimated support or resistance levels. When trading volume spikes, it can validate a potential bounce back, thus establishing a support or resistance line, or a break in such lines.

Now, this isn't a perfect system for identifying exact support and resistance levels. What this gives you, however, is a more objective and less random way to identify possible support and resistance zones. Support and resistance levels are rarely, if at all, exact.

Now that you understand a much better way to establish support and resistance levels, you can use this as one of your swing trading strategies, with confirmation from one or two more strategies or indicators, of course. How?

1. During a bullish trend, you can consider shorting a security or closing a long position on it when it busts through a seemingly established support line accompanied by significantly heavier trading volume. This may signal a reversal into a bearish trend already.

2. During a bearish trend, consider taking a long position or closing a short position on a security when prices break above the established resistance level accompanied by substantially heavier trading volume. It's highly possible that the bearish trend has already reversed into a bullish one.

Chapter 3

The Channel Swing Trading Strategy

This swing trading strategy's one of the best ways to swing your way to profits. It's because apart from its cunning accuracy, it's also one of the easiest and most intuitive swing trading strategies you can use.

The really good news about most financial securities and markets is that they usually trade within a price band between 20% and 25%. This makes swing trading with this strategy easy to use with high potential for good profits.

The Price Channel Pattern

This particular pattern is created by two trend lines that are nearly parallel. The line above is the resistance line, while the one below is the support line. In a price channel pattern, price action's constrained within the two trend lines.

To take advantage of price channel patterns for swing trading, they need to be wide enough to provide potentially good swing trading profits. There are two ways you can use the price channel pattern for swing trading.

The first way is to buy at or near the channel's support line and sell at or near the resistance line. Pretty simple, huh?

The second way you can use the price channel pattern for swing trading profits is through price breakouts. These can create substantial price swings opposite the existing trend, which can provide excellent swing trading profit opportunities.

There are three general types of price channels: upward, downward, and sideways channels. An upward channel is one where succeeding highs and lows are higher. And consistent with channel patterns, prices move between the upward-sloping support and resistance lines connecting those increasing high and low prices. And when the price breaks out of these support or resistance lines, it's a trigger for taking or closing positions.

The Underlying Principle behind the Price Channel Swing Trading Strategy

You can minimize your swing trading losses if you clearly understand the market psychology underlying the Price Channel strategy. The primary reason why price channel breakouts can lead to significant price swings is due to the fact that a lot of traders trade within the channel. Most of them execute stop-loss orders above and below a price channel's resistance and support levels, respectively.

As the stop-loss orders accumulate outside a price channel pattern, smart money traders will eventually try and take advantage of these stop-loss orders. The reason for this is such massive stop-loss orders provide liquidity, which many smart money traders also need.

One thing you'll need to understand about price channel swing trading: all price channels are temporary, and price channel breakouts will eventually happen. The only question is: When will the breakouts happen?

Since most swing traders, especially beginners, aren't qualified to take short-selling positions, the assumption is that swing trading involves buying and selling of financial securities only. As such, we'll talk about the channels as follows:

The Price Channel Swing Trading Strategy –Selling

Step #1: Draw the Price Channel

First, draw a price channel when there's a minimum of two higher highs (HH) and higher lows (HL). Draw the resistance and support lines by simply connecting the higher highs and higher lows, respectively.

At this point, the goal is to identify distinct price actions that move within the channel, which are formed by the support and resistance lines you'll draw.

Step #2: Wait Until the Last Price Swing Fails to Hit the Upper Limit of the Price Channel

Particularly for an upward or bullish trending price channel pattern, a very telling sign that a price breakout from the channel's support line is imminent is when a security's most recent price swing fails to reach the upper limit of the channel, i.e., the resistance line. This indicates that the upward price momentum's beginning to lose steam and a trend reversal may be confirmed by an eventual falling through of prices below the channel's support line.

Keep in mind that the higher the number of times that an upward price swing fails to reach the channel's resistance or upper band, the higher the likelihood of a downward price breakout.

Step #3: Wait for the Downward Price Breakout to Happen and for a Confirmation

To minimize your risks for a false breakout signal or "whiplash," you'll need to do something else aside from wait for an actual price breakout to happen; wait for a confirmation signal for the said breakout. But what is a confirmation signal?

In particular, we're talking about Japanese candlesticks, particularly a Japanese candlestick breakout whose closing price is below the channel's support line. In short, don't just sell immediately as soon as a security's price falls below the channel's support line. Ideally, the Japanese breakout candlestick should look decisively big, though it isn't compulsory.

Step #4: Sell

Once you've confirmed the price channel breakout, it's time to sell your security at the Japanese candle's closing price.

It's that easy.

Setting Profit Targets with Fibonacci Retracement

This swing trading strategy can be used in conjunction with other swing trading strategies, including the Fibonacci retracement strategy.

For example, you can set your first profit-taking point at the 23.6% retracement level of the previous trend, the second profit-taking point at the 38.2%, and the third (should you choose to have one) at the 61.8% retracement level.

You may be wondering what the "previous" trend is. Well, it's the trend contained within the price channel pattern from which the price has broken out of.

Setting Stop Loss Orders

It's better to err on the side of caution, as the saying goes. While losses are inevitable at some point during your swing trading activities, you can minimize their amounts through automatic stop-loss orders.

As mentioned earlier, many swing traders set their stop-loss limits or orders outside of price channels, i.e., above the resistance lines or below the support lines. You can do this, too. But if you want to err on the side of caution, you might want to try and set your limits to above the last significant upward price swing.

Final Words

The Price Channel Swing Trading strategy can be used in any financial market trading activity, e.g., stocks, bonds, currencies, etc.

Keep in mind that one of the most telling signs of a potential price breakout or reversal is multiple failures to reach one of the channel's limits, i.e., upper or lower. When you see such failures, get ready to execute your swing trade.

Chapter 4

The Breakout Swing Trading Strategy

B reakout trading is a swing trading strategy that times trades when a security's price moves beyond an established price range for that security. Price ranges have upper and lower limits represented by resistance and support lines/levels, respectively.

Before discussing this swing trading strategy in greater details, it's important to know the two main kinds of breakouts: support and resistance breakouts and swing high and low breakouts. Let's talk about support and resistance breakouts first.

As you can probably glean from its name, these types of breakouts refer to incidents when a security's price moves significantly beyond a price range's established support and resistance levels. That's why it's important that you become very familiar with objectively drawing support and resistance lines, which was discussed in the support-resistance swing trading strategy.

When prices go out of an established price range or channel, is it already a breakout? When employing this swing trading strategy, you'll need to identify legitimate breakouts from fake ones. A legitimate breakout is one that's immediately followed by a large, bold Japanese candlestick, which closes significantly above or below a price range's resistance or support level, respectively. When it comes to breakout trading, the larger the Japanese breakout candlestick is, the better.

When prices break out of the upper limit, it's a good time to take long positions or close short ones. When the breakout of the lower limit, it's a good time to take short positions or close long ones.

Now, what about swing high and low breakouts? It works similar to the support and resistance breakout strategy, save for an extra filter. And that filter is set up to provide the highest chances for a profitable trade. You see, not all swing highs and swing lows are the same, i.e., some are better than others while some are worse than others.

For purposes of swing high and low breakout trading, we'll focus on one set up that works very well for many swing traders: the V-shape swing. A V-shape swing high is characterized by a very strong price climb that's immediately succeeded by a very strong sell-off, i.e., a substantial price drop. For price swing lows, a V-shape swing is characterized by a substantial price drop immediately followed by a strong price climb or rally.

It's tempting to want to believe that you can use breakout trading as your only swing trading strategy and profit happily ever after. Sorry to burst your bubble but that's a bad idea because breakout trading can produce a lot of whiplashes or false breakout signals. That's why you'll need to pair it with another technical indicator, one that you can use as a confirmation tool. What's this technical indicator?

It's the volume-weighted moving average or VWMA. As the last three words indicate, it's an exponential or weighted moving average, where each price entry has a different weight in the computation of the moving average. Unlike the EMA, however, the VWMA considers trading volume – not recency – as the basis for assigning weights to the price data components used in computing the average. While the EMA puts the heaviest weight on the most recent price and the least weight on the oldest one, the VWMA puts the heaviest weight on the price with the most trading volume and puts the least weight on the one with the lowest trading volume.

Now that you're aware of the need to use the VWMA for the breakout swing trading strategy, it's time to get right into the strategy.

Breakout Strategy for Taking Long Positions or Closing Short Ones

The first step is to identify either a V-shaped swing high. Once you do, mark that specific high price level as a resistance level, from which you'll draw a horizontal line. The point of doing this is to identify and recognize only those price levels that are both clear and significant.

The next step is to patiently wait until the security's price eventually breaks through that resistance level and its Japanese candlestick closes above that resistance level. That's the significant breakout you should wait for, which is a signal that the bullish traders have seized control from the bearish ones.

But wait...there's more! We need a final confirmation to really trust that the breakout is legit: the VWMA! When the VWMA confirms the breakout, that's your "buy" go signal! In particular, the breakout should happen with the security's VWMA stretching upward and leaning more towards a continued upside movement.

Once you've taken your position, place your stop-loss order for this trade at a price that's slightly below the breakout Japanese candlestick. Then, place your profit-taking order immediately or if you want to feel the market, when the security's price breaks below its VWMA.

A VWMA-oriented profit-taking strategy is based on the idea that when a price goes below the VWMA, it's highly likely that the rally-sustaining buyers may have already run out. The logic here is to lock in on profits before the security's price completely starts to rollover.

Breakout Strategy for Taking Long Positions or Closing Short Ones

The strategy here is the complete inverse of the one for taking long positions or closing short ones.

The first step is to identify either a V-shaped swing slow. Once you do, mark that specific low price level as a support level, from which you'll draw a horizontal line.

The next step is to patiently wait until the security's price eventually breaks below that resistance level and its Japanese candlestick closes below that support level. That's the significant breakout you should wait for, which is a signal that the bearish traders have seized control from the bulls.

When the VWMA confirms the breakout, that's your "sell" go signal! In particular, the breakout should happen with the security's VWMA plunging downward and leaning more towards a continued drop.

Final Words on the Breakout Swing Trading Strategy

One of the best things about using this strategy is that your trades are backed up by price momentum. This gives you a very good chance of executing more profitable trades than losing ones.

Another benefit to using this strategy is immediate feedback. You'll quickly learn if your breakout trading strategy will or will not work.

And lastly, consider the possibility of breakouts being driven by institutional investors' money. That may give a price breakout even more confirmation and support.

Chapter 5

The Simple Moving Average (SMA) Strategy

Moving averages are one of the most popular technical analysis tools since time immemorial. There are several kinds of moving averages but the easiest to understand and use is the simple moving average or the SMA.

A moving average refers to the average price of a financial security for the last number of time periods, e.g., minutes, hours, days, weeks, months, etc. The reason it's called moving is that the time period used to calculate the average prices move. For example, the 5-day average price of Stock A at the open of April 6 is the average of its closing prices from April 1 to April 5. On the other hand, the 5-day average opening price for April 7 would be the average closing price from April 2 to April 6, which is different from April 6's. In effect, the time frame for computing the average moves forward as time goes on, hence the term "moving average."

The easiest type of moving the average to compute is the simple one. It's just the mathematical average of the last X number of trading periods. These average prices are plotted on the same chart as the actual prices of the securities concerned to create a moving average that runs above or below the actual price charts. Unlike actual price charts, moving average lines have a "smooth" appearance, i.e., no peaks and troughs. It's for this reason that moving averages are also referred to as price action smoothers that help traders more easily identify trends and reversals.

Simple moving averages, or moving averages in general, are used for identifying trend directions and reversals. The most common SMAs used by traders include:

10 SMA, i.e., 10-period moving average;

20 SMA, i.e., 20-period moving average;

50 SMA, i.e., 50- period moving average; and

100 SMA, i.e., 100-period moving average.

In an upward trending security, prices are going up, which means that the average prices moving forward are also increasing. This results in a smooth and upward-sloping SMA line. On the other hand, a downward trending security's average prices are generally going down, resulting in a smooth and downward sloping SMA line.

Using SMAs for Swing Trading

You can use the SMA as a versatile swing trading strategy in conjunction with one or two more or as a stand-alone swing trading tool for identifying current trends and reversals for timing your swing trades.

When you plot moving average prices for the same time period, the shorter-period SMA will always be higher than a longer-period one during a bullish or upward trend. The opposite is true during bearish or downward trends, i.e., the shorter-period SMA is always lower than the longer-period one.

Now, what's the significance of this? When a shorter-period SMA becomes lower than a longer-period one, it means that an upward trend has reversed and the security is now in a down trend. When the opposite happens, i.e., the shorter-period exceeds the longer-period SMA, this signifies that a bearish or downward trend has ended and an upward one has already begun.

When the end of a bearish trend and the start of a bullish one has been confirmed by a shorter-period SMA going above a longer-period one, it's a signal to take a long position on that security. Later, when the shorter-period SMA goes below the longer-period one, it confirms the start of a bearish trend and signals that you need to close your open position on the security, i.e., sell them already.

Further, crossover trading signals must be accompanied by a Japanese Candlestick that closes between the shorter and longer-period moving averages. The Japanese Candlestick is a confirmatory signal that will give you the go-ahead signal to trade accordingly.

Despite what many traders may say or do, you should never, ever use moving averages, simple or otherwise, as support and resistance lines. Why?

Because they're mathematical computations that indicate the average price of a security for the last several time periods, they do not really support or resistance lines. Although there are instances that moving averages look like strong support and resistance levels, these are just coincidences.

In summary, here are the key points for using SMAs for swing trading:

1. Take positions consistent with the trend your SMAs identify via crossovers.

2. When the shorter-period SMA crosses above the longer-period one, it means that a bullish or upward trend has begun. When the shorter-period SMA crosses below the longer-period one, it means that a bearish or a downward trend has begun.

3. When a Japanese Candlestick closes between the shorter and longer-period SMAs, it's a confirmation of a crossover trend reversal and a trading signal, i.e., buy or sell.

4. Moving averages, in and by themselves, aren't trading rules or signals. It's best to use at least two moving average periods to identify trend reversals and a Japanese Candlestick to confirm such identified reversals before taking or closing your swing trading positions.

Chapter 6

The Moving Average Convergence Divergence (MACD) Strategy

Now that you're familiar with the concept of moving averages, it's time to take it up a notch by learning the swing trading strategy called moving average convergence divergence or MACD.

What makes it different from the SMA earlier? First, MACD uses a different kind of moving average, i.e., the exponential moving average or EMA. Unlike the SMA, which grants equal weight for all prices used to compute the average, the EMA gives more weight to the most recent prices and less weight to the earlier ones.

The SMA simply averages the prices for a specific time period. A simple average assigns the same weight for all the prices, i.e., it divides the sum total of the prices by the number of time periods. By simply dividing the sum total of prices by the number of time periods, it gives each price the same contribution to the total.

Let's consider the following prices for the last ten trading days of Stock A:

- Day 1 (the earliest price period): $5.00
- Day 2: $5.50
- Day 3: $5.35
- Day 4: $5.40
- Day 5: $5.25

- Day 6: $5.35
- Day 7: $5.80
- Day 8: $5.65
- Day 9: $5.30
- Day 10 (Yesterday, the latest price period): $5.10

The simple average formula, which is what the SMA uses, is:

$$SMA = \Sigma \text{ Prices} \div \text{\# of Price Periods}$$

Using the prices above:

$$\Sigma \text{ Prices} = \$5.00 + \$5.50 + \$5.35 + \$5.40 + \$5.25 + \$5.35 + \$5.80 + \$5.65 + \$5.30 + \$5.10$$

$$\Sigma \text{ Prices} = \$53.70$$

$$\text{\# of Price Periods} = 10$$

$$SMA = \$53.70 \div 10$$

$$SMA = \$5.37$$

Another way you can express this equation to show the equal weights given to all prices is this:

$$SMA = \Sigma \text{ (Prices} \times 1 \div \text{\# of Price Periods)}$$

Using the same prices from earlier:

- Day 1: $5.00 ÷ 10 = $0.500
- Day 2: $5.50 ÷ 10 = $0.550
- Day 3: $5.35 ÷ 10 = $0.535
- Day 4: $5.40 ÷ 10 = $0.540
- Day 5: $5.25 ÷ 10 = $0.525
- Day 6: $5.35 ÷ 10 = $0.535

- Day 7: $5.80 ÷ 10 = $0.580
- Day 8: $5.65 ÷ 10 = $0.565
- Day 9: $5.30 ÷ 10 = $0.530
- Day 10: $5.10 = $0.510

$$SMA = \Sigma\ (Prices \times 1 \div \#\ of\ Price\ Periods)$$

Because it's a simple average where all prices have equal weights, each of them has a weight of 10%, or 1÷10.

Using this iteration of the SMA formula, we get:

- Day 1: $5.00 X 10% = $0.500
- Day 2: $5.50 X 10%= $0.550
- Day 3: $5.35 X 10% = $0.535
- Day 4: $5.40 X 10% = $0.540
- Day 5: $5.25 X 10% = $0.525
- Day 6: $5.35 X 10% = $0.535
- Day 7: $5.80 X 10% = $0.580
- Day 8: $5.65 X 10% = $0.565
- Day 9: $5.30 X 10% = $0.530
- Day 10: $5.10 X 10% = $0.510

The sum total of these prices is:

SMA = $5.37

This kind of averaging assumes that the oldest prices are just as relevant as the latest ones. The EMA assumes that the latest prices are more relevant when it comes to trends and hence, it gives more weight to the latest prices and less weight to the oldest ones.

There are many ways to assign weights for prices in an EMA series but for purposes of a simple discussion, let's assign the following weights to the ten prices in our example. Take note that the total sum of the weights should equal 1 or 100%.

- Day 1: $5.00 X 15% = $0.750
- Day 2: $5.50 X 13%= $0.715
- Day 3: $5.35 X 12% = $0.642
- Day 4: $5.40 X 11% = $0.594
- Day 5: $5.25 X 10% = $0.525
- Day 6: $5.35 X 9% = $0.482
- Day 7: $5.80 X 8.50% = $0.493
- Day 8: $5.65 X 8.00% = $0.452
- Day 9: $5.30 X 7.50% = $0.398
- Day 10: $5.10 X 6.00% = $0.306

The sum total of these weighted prices is $5.356 or $5.36, which is slightly lower than the SMA. This is because the last two trading days saw a plunge in Stock A's price and because the last two trading days carried the most weight, it brought the EMA down to less than the SMA. In a sense, it reflects market sentiment and momentum better than the SMA because the last few trading days are a better reflection of current market sentiment compared to the prices 9 to 10 days ago.

So, how does the MACD really work apart from using EMA instead of SMA? The MACD is more of a momentum indicator than a trend indicator. It tells you when a certain trend is gaining, losing, or has no more momentum. If the SMA identifies trends and reversals, the MACD is a lagging indicator that follows trends and measures their momentum strength, the default values of which are 9, 12, and 26.

Aside from using the EMA, it also features a histogram to show trend momentum strength.

Because of the words "moving average" in the term, many traders tend to confuse the MACD with the SMA and consequently its trading strategy. To avoid confusion, you should keep in mind that MACD uses EMAs, which tend to react more to the latest price actions compared to the SMA. The MACD lines are usually 12-period and 26-period EMAs.

Just like SMA lines, EMA lines are relatively smooth compared to actual price charts as it uses average figures instead of exact ones. There are two colored EMA lines when plotting MACD: a blue and a red line.

The blue line represents the difference between the 12-period and 26-period EMAs. The red line represents the 9-day EMA of a security, which is considered as the trigger line. It's called as such because when the blue line crosses it, it means that price momentum has shifted.

In an upward trending market, the blue line is above the red line, which indicates an upward price momentum. When the blue line crosses below the red line, it means that price momentum has shifted to a downward momentum.

At the bottom of every MACD chart is a histogram, the values are shown on which is either above zero (positive) or below zero (negative). When the blue line's above the red line, the histogram value for that period is positive or above the zero line. When below the red line, the histogram's value for that period is negative, i.e., below the zero line. This indicates the strength of a security's momentum.

Traders use different time-period lengths for the trigger line other than the 9-period. Here's something to consider when choosing the duration of your trigger line: the shorter the duration, the more sensitive your triggers will be and vice versa. With greater sensitivity, however, comes a greater chance of encountering whiplashes or false signals. It's because the more sensitive a trigger line is, the more signals it will generate, many of which may be whiplashes only.

A less sensitive trigger line may have much lower risks for whiplashes and may thus be more accurate. However, the tradeoff with a very long trigger is delayed triggers, which can put you at risk of missing on good trading opportunities because of slow ability to catch shifts in momentum.

How do you choose the most appropriate trigger line duration? I'd say it's best just to use your trading platform's default MACD settings and see how it works for you in the first few weeks or months. During this period, you can observe if the default is too sensitive (many whiplashes), insensitive (you miss out on many trading opportunities), or just about right. Then, adjust accordingly, if needed.

MACD Trading Signals

The only signal you'll need to concern yourself with when it comes to trading using the MACD swing trading strategy is when the blue line (the MACD line) crosses below and above the red line (the trigger line). And when it comes to using the MACD for trading signals, you don't need to have a substantial line-crossing just to validate trading signals.

The only thing you'll need to watch out for is when the trigger line and the MACD lines cross and the direction by which they cross. It'll give you a clear idea that a possible trend in the cross' direction might be emerging based on momentum shift.

One important thing you should consider about line crossings is this: you shouldn't act on every trend line crossing. You'll have to qualify it.

When the MACD histogram is *below the zero value line*, which means the trigger (red) line is *above the MACD (blue) line*, do not maintain long positions in that security. It's because these indicate a downward price momentum and taking long positions during this time will most likely lead to swing trading losses. If your account and experience allow it, you may take short positions instead.

On the other hand, if the trigger (red) line is below the MACD (blue) line, then the MACD histogram value will be above the zero value line, which means an upward price momentum. This is a good time to either close a short position or take a long one in financial security.

When the MACD and the Security's Price Take Different Routes

There will be times when a security's price continues to register higher highs (HH) while its MACD histogram registers lower highs (LH). This is known as a bearish divergence.

There'll also be times when a security's price continues to register lower lows (LL) while the MACD histogram's value registers higher low (HL). This referred to as a bullish divergence.

How do you handle this? Wait and see if this persists. A reversal may not be imminent after one or two instances of divergence, but if it continues to persist, it might happen soon. The thing is not to jump on the reversal bandwagon way ahead of it happening. You may consider divergences as signals to stay alert for possible, imminent reversals.

Using MACD as an Overbought or Oversold Indicator

Just because the MACD doesn't have lower or upper limits doesn't mean you can't use it as an indicator of a security's already being overbought or oversold. If you want to use the MACD as an indicator of such, check the size of the gap in between the trigger and MACD lines.

Experts say that the greater the gap between the trigger and MACD lines, the stronger the current trend is and the chances of it continuing are higher, too. This means the longer the bars of the MACD histogram is, the stronger the current momentum is. It may indicate that the security isn't overbought or oversold yet, depending on the trend's direction.

On the other hand, when the gap between the trigger and MACD lines become narrower, it means that the momentum is weakening or already weak. This would mean that the length of the MACD histogram bars also become shorter, which indicates a lower probability of the current trend persisting. It may indicate that the security is already overbought or oversold or is close to becoming that, depending on the trend's direction.

Either way, the size of the gap between the red and blue lines and the length or height of the histogram bars can give you a heads up of a potentially impending trend reversal. Just keep in mind that because there are no numerical limits to MACD's values, you may have to go back a bit longer on a security's historical price to get a better estimate if a security's approaching an overbought or oversold position already.

MACD Swing Trading Combo Strategies

While using the MACD can give you relatively good swing trading success, using it in conjunction with other technical analysis tools may provide even better results. Keep in mind that while these MACD combo trading strategies have worked for many, it doesn't mean they're perfect and will work for you, too. Only that given the relative swing trading successes that many traders have experienced with these, they're worth trying out. As you go along, you can make the necessary adjustments as needed.

MACD Combo Swing Trading Strategy #1: With the Relative Vigor Index

The relative vigor index, or RVI, is an oscillating technical indicator that focuses more on the relationship between a security's closing price and price range. Computing for the RVI is akin to rocket science and since trading platforms can generate this index for you without breaking a sweat, let's just focus on the logic behind using it in conjunction with the MACD.

Oscillators, or oscillating technical indicators, are measures of a security's overbought or oversold position. The MACD estimates a current trend's strength and consequently, gives you an idea of the likelihood that a trend will continue. The way these two work together is by matching their crossovers.

When either the MACD or the RVI registers a crossover, you'll have to wait for the other to register its own crossover in the same direction before taking positions in a security. Then, you'll rely on the MACD for signals to close your positions in that security.

MACD Combo Swing Trading Strategy #2: With the Money Flow Index

More commonly referred to by its acronym MFI, the money flow index is also an oscillator. However, this one focuses on price and trading volume instead of on price alone.

MFIs tend to generate fewer trading signals because it requires more information to create significant price readings, i.e., surges in trading volume and price movements. Just like the MACD + RVI combo strategy, you'll rely on crossovers from both indicators to take positions in a security.

In this combo, the lead indicator is the MFI. When a security's MFI indicates the security is already overbought, you don't act immediately. Instead, you'll have to wait for its MACD indicator to manifest a bearish crossover to either short the security or close an existing long position in the security.

On the other hand, when the MFI of a security indicates that it's already oversold, wait for the MACD's bullish crossover before taking a long position or closing a short one in that security. The main idea is to hold your horses when the MFI indicates overbought or oversold levels until the MACD exhibits the applicable crossover before taking or closing positions.

MACD Combo Swing Trading Strategy #3: With the Triple Exponential Moving Average

Abbreviated as TEMA, the triple exponential moving average indicator is – you guessed it right – an exponential moving average indicator! But wait, there's more: it doesn't just use one or two EMAs but three!

Because it uses three EMAs, validation occurs after two crossovers instead of just one. Now, if that's not enough validation of a trend reversal, I don't know what is!

Just like the SMA, shorter-period averages tend to produce a lot of trading signals and with it comes to a lot of whiplashes or false signals, too. That's why it's important to use periods that are long enough to minimize whiplashes but not too long that it gives trading signals too late in the game.

So, how do you use both the MACD and the TEMA on the same security? Your trading cues will come when the MACD lines crossover and the security's price breaks through the TEMA. To be more specific:

1. When the MACD (blue) line *crosses above* the trigger (red) line, and the security's Japanese Candlestick *closes above* the TEMA, it means the momentum is now upward, and it's time to either *take a long position or close a short one* in that security.

2. When the MACD (blue) line *crosses below* the trigger (red) line, and the security's Japanese Candlestick *closes below* the TEMA, it means the momentum is now downward, and it's time to either *take a short position or close a long one* in that security.

Because the TEMA can create more trading signals when the market's choppy, it's a good idea to pair it up with the MACD, which can smooth the ride and identify trading signals that have the greatest potential for swing trading profits.

148

MACD Combo Swing Trading Strategy #4: With the TRIX Indicator

TRIX is yet another technical oscillator but to be more specific; it's a trend and momentum oscillator. It specifically measures the rate of change – of momentum – of a TEMA. It generates two trading signals: signal line crossovers and divergences.

How do you use both indicators to strategize or time your swing trades? Wait for the MACD and the trigger lines to crossover and for the TRIX indicator to cross the zero level. When these two cross overs match, it's a signal to take the appropriate positions and wait for the security to start trending to your advantage:

1. When the MACD (blue) line *crosses above* the trigger (red) line, and when the TRIX indicator *crosses above the zero level, take a long position or close a short one* in that security; and

2. When the MACD (blue) line *crosses below* the trigger (red) line, and when the TRIX indicator *crosses below the zero level, take a short position or close a long one* in that security.

MACD Combo Swing Trading Strategy #5: With the Awesome Oscillator

The Awesome Oscillator (AO) is one that has no limits. Maybe that's why it's awesome! But seriously, the AO is simply the difference between two simple moving averages – a 5-period and a 34-period SMA.

Here's how to use the MACD and the AO to time your swing trades well:

1. When the MACD (blue) line *crosses above* the trigger (red) line, and when the AO *crosses above the zero level, take a long position or close a short one* in that security; and

149

2. When the MACD (blue) line *crosses below* the trigger (red) line, and when the AO indicator *crosses below the zero level, take a short position or close a long one* in that security.

Chapter 7

The 5-Step Swing Trade Test

Regardless of the financial securities you trade, e.g., stocks, cryptocurrencies, etc., trading opportunities abound once the opening bell sounds. But the question to ponder is, are those opportunities worth taking advantage of? In short, what's the probability of profiting from available trading opportunities?

As mentioned earlier, none of the strategies presented earlier are perfect. Each of them has their own strengths and weaknesses. And while many have sworn by those strategies, it may take time before newbie or intermediate swing traders get the hang of them such that they profit from their trades most of the time.

As a newbie or intermediate trader, what are you to do while you're still feeling the ropes? Don't worry, here are five important steps to "test" the trading opportunities available to you so you can have a very good idea of their potential profitability. After you've practiced these five steps enough, you'll need but a few seconds to execute them.

The Set-Up

This step refers to identifying specific conditions that can optimize your chances of swing trading profitably. If you're using a trend-following strategy, a trend needs to be present obviously as a condition for making swing trading positions. Even more important, you must have established parameters or conditions for considering a particular trend as a tradable one. The ability to spot trends and evaluate whether they're tradable is a very essential set up if you employ a trend-following strategy, such as the MACD.

If the setup conditions you deem are important aren't there, don't make the trade. It's that simple. Following even just this one rule can save you a lot of emotional and financial stress.

The Trade Trigger

When the basic conditions for evaluating potentially profitable trades are present or laid out, you'll need a very specific and objective event, i.e., anything other than "gut feel," that will tell you to take positions now. Some examples of position-taking or trading triggers include:

1. After pulling back or ranging from new highs, e.g., correcting after breaching an important resistance level but still above it;

2. Price pullbacks, i.e., when a security's price pulls back to or near an established support area;

3. For Fibonacci Retracement traders, when prices hit important ratios, e.g., 23.6%, 38.2%, and 61.8%; and

4. For MACD and oscillator users, when indicators cross over or below their respective zero values.

The Stop-Loss Order

While having the ideal trading conditions present and having a relatively objective trading or position-taking trigger is very important, it's not enough to ensure a good trade. Since no trading strategy's perfect, the risk of loss always looms on the horizon. Hence, you must also have a sensible approach to managing your market risk, i.e., the risk of losing money due to unfavorable changes in a security's market price.

When it comes to market risk, you can't eliminate it, but you can manage it such that you can minimize your potential losses on trades.

The most common-sense approach to market risk management is a stop-loss order at a pre-determined price. This refers to trading orders placed in advance at specific prices that will compel the closing of a trade position to cut losses.

There are various ways to determine stop-loss order prices or triggers. These include:

1. Identifying the price at which your trading loss will be limited according to your maximum loss tolerance, in percentage terms or dollar amounts. For example, if your personal loss limit is 10% per trade, determine the lowest selling (for long positions) or highest buying (for short positions) price that will correspond to a maximum trading loss of 10%.

2. It is choosing a price that's just a wee bit below the most recent low price swing or support for long positions and for short ones, a price that's slightly above the most recent high price swing or resistance.

3. Choosing a stop-loss price within the vicinity of your trade's entry price based on a volatility measure called the Average True Range.

The Profit-Taking Target Price

Now that you have clear ideas of the conditions needed to execute your trading strategy as well as when to take positions and cut-them short to minimize losses, it's time to get clear on the main reason for your swing trading: profits! You should next set a profit-taking target price.

Why the need for a profit-taking price? If you don't set one up, there's a pretty good chance that greed will rear its ugly head and turn an already profitable trade (at least on paper) into a losing one. Let me share my horrible experience of not setting a profit-taking price beforehand during my newbie swing trading years.

Once I took a substantial long position in the stock of a well-known real estate company. I wasn't aware of the importance of setting profit-taking targets back then, so I just thought about when to exit on a daily basis.

After just a week or two, the stock's price went up such that my paper trading profits was already 15%. Not bad for a week's trade. But considering the market, in general, was upbeat, I decided 15% wasn't enough. I said to the stock market deity: "Please Sir, can I have some more?"

True enough, the price went up further the following week such that I was already up 30%. But greed continued to rear its ugly head, and I continued imploring the stock market deity for more.

The next two weeks, the price went down, but I was still up by 10%. The greed-devil in my mind continued whispering to me: it's just a correction, and it will resume its upward journey to even greater profits! It even convinced me to turn off all indicators just to justify the decision to keep my long position open.

Long story short, I ended up with a 20% trading loss instead as the market reversed into bear territory.

That's what can happen if you don't set profit-taking targets. Both profit-taking and stop-loss targets are essential to manage your risks and optimize your chances for a profitable trade.

You can set profit targets in two ways: based on gut-feel or based on established support and resistance levels. For example, if you took a long position at a price near the support line of a channel, consider setting a profit-taking target price near the top or support line of that channel.

Don't let greed rear its ugly head and turn potential gold into garbage.

The Risk-Reward Ratio

While the acceptable ratio may vary between traders depending on their risk appetite and profit goals, a good place to start is a 1.5 ratio, i.e., your estimated potential reward for the trade should be at least 1.5 times the possible loss. For example, if a trade has the potential to lose $100, it should also have the potential to make you at least $150 if things go well.

How do you determine the risk-reward ratio of your trade? A good and easy way to do it is by looking at your entry, stop-loss, and profit-taking target prices. The difference between your target entry and stop-loss prices is the risk component of the ratio, and the difference between your target entry and profit-taking prices is the reward component. Divide the reward component by the risk component, and you get you risk-reward ratio.

If a potential trade you're eyeing up has a risk-reward ratio of lower than your established one, e.g., 1.5, don't make the trade. Remember, half of your swing trading success lies in your ability to avoid swing trades with high risks for trading losses.

Other Things to Consider

The five steps outlined above function as filters that can help you sift high loss potential trades from the high-profit potential ones. These are general principles that you can use with the trading strategies outlined in this book so you can maximize your profit potential and minimize your risks for loss.

But as with all other trading strategies, these aren't perfect. There will always be some trades that may pass these filters but end up giving you losses. That's alright because if you do your homework right,

Step 3 – Stop-Loss Orders – will be there to make sure your losses are tolerable and won't impair your ability to continue swing trading.

The 5-Step Conclusion

Before executing any swing trading strategy, make sure that the conditions are suitable for taking positions. Then, employ objective triggers, like crossovers or retracement levels, as signals that will tell you when to take positions. And before you act on those triggers, determine beforehand what your stop-loss and profit-taking prices will be so that you avoid trading on emotions, which can be very dangerous as you've seen in my example earlier. Finally, determine – based on your target entry, stop-loss, and profit-taking prices – the potential trades' risk-reward ratio. If it's less than your ideal, e.g., 1.5, don't make the trade and look for others that will meet your ratio.

In the beginning, this can take you a couple of minutes to complete. But as you continue practicing these five steps, you'll become so adept at it that you'll be able to complete them in under a minute.

Final Words

Important Things to Keep in Mind

Before you go and start applying the swing trading strategies you just learned, I want you to keep a couple of very important things in mind. Call them general guiding principles, if you will, that applies regardless of the strategy you choose. Keeping them in mind and following them will help you optimize your chances of successfully executing swing trades.

Get in Early in the Game

While there's no rule prohibiting you from taking positions after a trend has already charted its course, the later you come in, the lower your chances of executing profitable trades. On the other hand, the earlier you catch a trend and get to ride it by taking a position, you have a much longer profit potential period and consequently, higher chances for higher trading profits.

The key here is to always be on top of the overall market's averages. Remember, most securities follow their specific market's general direction. So, when the market's averages indicate overbought and/or oversold levels, chances of a trend reversal are imminent.

Trade in the General Direction of the Market Only

When it comes to U.S. stocks, the best measurement for the stock market's overall direction may be the S&P 500 index. The trend of this index can give you context for making short-term trading moves, such as the case with swing trading.

Why go with the general direction of the market for swing trading? If the general, longer-term trend of the market is going upward, the chances of a security's price following suit, especially in the short term, are much higher than going the opposite direction. The same is true if the general market's bearish. The only exception is when there's a major event or development specific to that security, which can provide enough impetus for traders to trade it in the opposite direction as the market.

Consider a Longer Trading Time Frame

As a swing trader, the most you'll be holding on to a position is a couple of months – and that's already long by swing trading standards. But that doesn't mean you should only base your swing trading decisions on short-term trends.

When you simply focus on short-term trends, prices, and indicators, you'll end up with a limited or incomplete analysis or evaluation of a security's possible price actions. It's because you won't be able to see the entire picture or context in which the trend is located.

During bear markets, there'll always be short periods when prices of securities tend to go up in the short term as part of the correction phase. If you focused solely on the short-term trend, you might be tempted to believe that such uptrends are very solid ones and will most likely hold. But if you're aware of the greater context, you'll see that those are corrections and will most likely end sooner than you think.

Remember, look at the longer picture, i.e., intermediate-term, even if you're just swing trading, which is short term in nature.

Never Rely on Just One Indicator

I mentioned this several times in this book, but it's worth repeating one final time. It's like buying an online course from a person you hardly know. You look for legitimate product reviews, and the more positive reviews you read about the course, the higher the likelihood that the course is a legit and solid one. And based on such likelihood, you'll probably enroll in that online course, even if it's a bit pricey.

While you don't need to get that many indicators to confirm the validity of a trading signal, it's still important to use two to three indicators to generate/confirm a trading signal, especially if you use indicators that use different underlying principles and ideas to generate trading signals. If different methodologies and principles generate the same signal for a security, the chances are that it's a legit one.

Use Multiple Time-Frames for Charts

This idea follows that of the previous one: multiple confirmations of the same thing.

When you analyze daily, weekly, and monthly charts for the same period for a security, you may or may not recognize a pattern that can tell you a clear story of that security. For example, do most or all of the time frame charts show trend reversal or continuation confirmations from volume or momentum indicators? Do they generally hold true for most, if not all, time frames used? The more consistent it is across different time frames, the stronger your analysis will be.

Never Take Positions without a Good Trading Plan

Failing to plan is – as cliché as it may sound – planning to fail. Same goes for your swing trading. If you don't set entry points, stop-loss and profit-taking targets, and re-entry points, you'll end up swing trading on impulse or emotion. Remember my story earlier, where I let gold turn into garbage because of greed and trading based on emotions? Don't follow that example.

When it comes to successful swing trading, your ability to preserve your trading capital is of utmost importance. This is the importance of setting stop-loss limits, and the best time to do that is just before you execute a trade, not after. And more importantly, set your online trading account to automatically close your positions when your stop-loss limits are hit to ensure you really cut your losses and preserve your capital for another trading day. If not, instruct your broker to do it for you as soon as the stop-loss price is hit.

To optimize your chances of quickly closing positions, regardless if at the stop-loss or profit-taking prices, limit your swing trades to stocks that are very, very liquid or actively traded on a daily basis. A stop-loss or profit-taking order, even if automated, can be useless if the market for your security isn't very liquid or isn't traded heavily. It's because the lack of liquidity can keep you from immediately executing such orders at your desired price levels.

Use Fundamental Analysis to Swing Trade, Too

You might think the fundamental analysis is useless for swing trading because it doesn't give you trading signals or tell you when to buy or sell securities. If you do, I don't blame you because that's 100% correct. But while that's correct, it's not the complete picture.

While the fundamental analysis doesn't answer the question of "when" to buy or sell securities, it can help you shortlist the securities to focus on for swing trading. With literally thousands of financial securities and hundreds of stocks to choose from, you can't afford to monitor technical tools, charts, and indicators for all of them to identify swing trading opportunities.

You can use fundamental analysis to identify the most fundamentally sound securities and those that have real potential for growth in the future. Fundamental analysis takes a look securities with the intention of identifying those that are financially strong and profitable. Between

160

securities of companies with weak financials and those with strong ones, you can make the case that you can swing trade more profitably with the latter because chances are, trades on financially weak securities are nothing more than speculation or gambling.

While there are also lots of fundamental information you can use to evaluate a security's health and profitability, two of the most important areas fundamental analysis considers is profitability and leverage.

Profitability determines whether a company will be around for long and whether it can grow in the future. The more profitable a company is, the more likely the price of its security will appreciate over the long term. A losing company has no hope of surviving long, much less grow.

Some of the key ratios used to evaluate a security or company's profitability are:

1. Return on Equity (ROE);

2. Earnings-per-Share (EPS); and

3. Price-Earnings Ratio (P/E Ratio).

Leverage refers to how much of a company's assets are funded by capital and by debt. The more leveraged a company is, i.e., the more debt it has, the higher its risk for bankruptcy is. The most important ratios used to express leverage are:

1. Debt-to-Equity Ratio;

2. Current Ratio (Current Assets vis-a-vis Current Liabilities); and

3. Quick Ratio (Current Assets (without marketable securities) vis-a-vis Current Liabilities).

Conclusion

Thanks for buying this book. I hope that through this, you didn't just learn specific strategies for successful swing trading but were also encouraged to take action and start trading right away. After all, knowledge is just potential power, and knowing's just half the battle. Action turns knowledge into actual power and is the other half of a successful battle for swing trading profits.

You don't need to apply everything at once. Just use one strategy for the first week or two and when you're already familiar with it, consider applying another one until you're able to use two to three strategies comfortably. Take baby steps, and when it comes to trading, it's better to err on the side of caution, particularly in the beginning as you're still learning the ropes.

And finally, apply what you learned on your trading platforms simulator first. Do swing trades on paper first, i.e., simulated swing trades. That way, you get to experience making or losing money without actually risking real money. This gives you the opportunity to master the strategies prior to doing real trades.

Here's to your swinging success, my friend! Cheers!

References

https://investinganswers.com/articles/swing-tradings-11-commandments-top-strategies-technical-analysis

https://tradingsim.com/blog/exponential-moving-average/

https://tradingsim.com/blog/macd/

https://tradingstrategyguides.com/price-channel-pattern-strategy/

https://whatis.techtarget.com/definition/Fibonacci-sequence

https://www.beststockpickingservices.com/macd-swing-trading-indicator/

https://www.beststockpickingservices.com/macd-swing-trading-indicator/

https://www.cmcmarkets.com/en/trading-guides/how-to-swing-trade-stocks

https://www.cmcmarkets.com/en/trading-guides/how-to-swing-trade-stocks

https://www.eatsleeptrade.net/technical-indicators-macd

https://www.investopedia.com/articles/active-trading/090415/only-take-trade-if-it-passes-5step-test.asp

https://www.investopedia.com/articles/active-trading/091114/strategies-trading-fibonacci-retracements.asp

https://www.netpicks.com/simple-moving-average/

https://www.netpicks.com/support-resistance/

Made in the USA
Las Vegas, NV
18 February 2021

18124990R00095